Advance Praise for *Don't Change the Channel*

"You don't need to spend much time reading the newspaper or watching TV to know there is a lot of destructive, discouraging and ultimately sad stuff going on in the world today. Jenn Snyder's book is a wonderful reminder that much of what is going on in our world is positive and encouraging. And all of us have the opportunity to make a difference in someone's life.

So sit back and be prepared to be inspired as well as learning some practical tips on how to be a positive influence in another person's life."

—David Williams, President & Chief Executive Officer of Make-A-Wish Foundation® of America

"The cable news cameras bring stories of heartbreak and despair from every corner of the country to our living rooms far too often. While our emotions are often moved by these sad tales, rarely are we motivated to make a difference in the lives that have been altered and forever changed.

Jenn Snyder's reaction to her call serves as equal parts inspiration and instruction, and *Don't Change the Channel* serves as a great road map for others to make a difference when they find themselves similarly called to action."

—Mike Tirico, ESPN Sportscaster

"How do you get busy people to make a difference? Jenn Snyder's *Don't Change the Channel* is full of inspiring ideas and stories. From inspiring acts of kindness to organizing large fundraisers, Snyder shows how to move people to move mountains."

—Rich Karlgaard, Publisher, *Forbes Magazine*

"*Don't Change the Channel* shows that we all have the ability to affect change on any level. The key is finding your passion, your cause, and channeling your energy into action. It is a worthy challenge not only to ask yourself 'What can I do to help today,' but also to act upon it."
—Jim Tressel, Head Football Coach, Ohio State University

"My job brings me in contact with some of the world's most dedicated, focused, and talented people. Jenn Snyder fits in well with that group. Her mind is always working on a new concept, event or idea to make this world a better place. Relentlessly optimistic, her batteries never seen to run down.

Champions are not intimidated by the bunkers, the water hazards or the rough. Instead, they concentrate on the target. Jenn did that with Blake and his family, and she made magic happen."
—Jim Nantz, CBS Sports Commentator, and Best-selling Author

"Snyder's book is an inspiration to us all about how we can make a small or a large difference to change the world step-by-step. Knowing Jenn, I am constantly amazed at how, at her young age, she has been able to tap into the wisdom and the important gift in life of giving back.

Don't Change the Channel is the perfect road map for how every one of us ordinary people can take an event or something we are passionate about and do some good in the world."
—Lee Woodruff, ABC News, and best-selling author

dontchangethechannel
dontchangethechannel
dontchangethechannel
dontchangethechannel
dontchangethechannel
dontchangethechannel
dontchangethechannel
dontchangethechannel
dontchangethechannel
dontchangethechannel
dontchangethechannel
dontchangethechannel
dontchangethechannel
dontchangethechannel
dontchangethechannel
dontchangethechannel

dontchangethechannel
dontchangethechannel
dontchangethechannel
dontchangethechannel
dontchangethechannel
dontchangethechannel
dontchangethechannel
dontchangethechannel
dontchangethechannel
dontchangethechannel
dontchangethechannel
dontchangethechannel
dontchangethechannel
dontchangethechannel
dontchangethechannel

dontchangethechannel

Make the World a Better Place

by Jenn Snyder
with Betsy Thorpe

Foot Soldier Publishing

Foot Soldier Publishing
9450 Moss Plantation Ave N.W.
Concord, NC 28027

ISBN: 978-0-9830782-03-3

The events and experiences detailed herein are true and have been faithfully rendered as the author remembers them to the best of her ability.

Book design by ANGELA HARWOOD

For Lori.
May your infectious spirit live in all of us.

contents
contents
contents
contents
contents
contents
contents
contents
contents

Contents

chapter one
chapter one
chapter one
chapter one
chapter one
chapter one
chapter one
chapter one
chapter one
chapter one
chapter one

Seizing Life's
Moments

Our lives are made of millions of moments.

Some moments you're worried about what to feed your family for dinner. Sometimes you're working feverishly to meet a deadline at work. Some moments you stop to take a deep breath before moving on to another task. Sometimes you get stuck in a moment, wondering if things will always stay the same.

Not all moments can be life changing. But don't you wish more of them were?

We spend most of our lives seeking times of happiness and satisfaction to elevate us out of the daily grind, and wish the same for people around us. Often, though, we aren't sure what it is that we can do in order to bring feelings of accomplishment, purpose and pleasure into our lives. We worry that our free time is too limited to be able to find true fulfillment. Although it may seem counter-intuitive, spending time helping others find happiness is an action that can bring us true joy. After all, if we could recall a moment when we have known the reward of putting a smile on someone else's face, wouldn't that help us get through the challenging moments of life?

We have the power to change people's lives for the

better, and thus make our own better as well. But the question for millions is: When can we find the time to effect change among all of the other moments in our daily grind?

Everywhere we look people are suffering. On television, we see the heartbreak of poverty, hunger, war, and illness. Down the street we may have neighbors who have a chronically ill child. There are schools that are in need of basic resources – books for the libraries, computers, buildings, and more teachers.

We often think we don't have the time or even the knowledge to help. We don't give ourselves permission to create possibilities when we see needs. Here's the good news: being extraordinary for someone can be done in small chunks of your time. Everyday kindnesses, such as remembering to hold the door open for someone, or paying the bill for the person behind you in the drive-through, can make somebody's day.

The truth is, all of us have moments that we can harness and put to use for others. We just have to recognize them when they come and not look the other way.

All of us have moments that we can harness and put to use for others.

I wrote this book to help inspire people to seize moments in their lives to help others. In one moment, you can change someone's life forever. In one moment, you can change the world.

Blake's Bright Tomorrow

My moment came as I was sitting on the couch, watching CNN. I was following a heart-breaking case of a pregnant mother's disappearance in my hometown of Uniontown, Ohio. Emotionally tied to the case from the start, I had no idea at the time how much it would change my life. Thousands of people from our small town worked with national search organizations to scour the surrounding area to find the body of nine-months pregnant Jessie Davis.

Tears streamed from my eyes as I listened to the story of how Jessie's two-and-a-half-year-old son Blake was left alone in his house for two days until his grandmother discovered him. While I watched the news conference it was announced that Jessie's body had been found, and her boyfriend, the father to Blake and his unborn sister, was being charged with double murder.

In that moment, I knew I had to do something for this little boy whose life had been changed forever. I heard the call, felt the conviction and there was no turning away. There was no going back to my busy life without making an attempt to alleviate some of this family's suffering.

Once I seized the moment, a spark was ignited inside others and the movement grew. We created a swell of support that was a joy to be a part of.

From that moment on, I worked to try and make Blake's family's life less painful. Although nothing I could do would ever bring back Jessie or her unborn daughter Chloe, I could help Blake and his family have a brighter tomorrow. Within two weeks, I established a trust fund called "Blake's Bright Tomorrow," and with the help of many wonderful and inspiring people, we were able to raise money for Blake's college education, get a foreclosed house donated, and hold a community-wide fundraising event. Within four months, the house was gutted, renovated, and stocked full of food and furniture for Blake and his family. Today, they live in that beautiful house.

People are amazed that those of us who worked on Blake's Bright Tomorrow could have gotten so much accomplished so quickly. It is possible to accomplish so much if you are passionate about a cause, get organized with a plan, team up with energetic people, and get the word out. Imagine what would happen if everyone decided to turn their energies into trying to make things better for others, instead of throwing up their hands and hoping things get better on their own.

There was no changing the channel for me that night – I was focused in on the cause. Until I had figured out a way to help make this little boy's future look brighter, I knew I could not rest. I made it a mission to get as many people around the country committed to this cause as I could. I worked countless hours to pull this event together.

The idea of holding a community-wide festival and fund-raiser would accomplish two tasks: one, bring the community together to support this family and help the healing process, and two, raise money for Blake to help insure a brighter future with the help of a college education. Although I was living and running a business 500 miles away from my hometown, I was determined that time and distance were not going to stand in my way.

I started to get the word out and made phone calls. A friend and I sat at her kitchen table and thought up the name: Blake's Bright Tomorrow. I needed a place in our community that would be large and central enough to hold the festival. For me, there was one place in my hometown I wanted to have it. It's the cornerstone of our community – the Hartville Kitchen, which sits on many acres of land. I was so excited and grateful when they donated their land for this purpose. I had a place, a date, and time for the event – it was to take place three weeks after that news conference I saw on CNN.

Ann Kagarise, a reporter from a local newspaper, had been covering the story from the beginning. She called when she heard what I was doing. During our conversation, she shared with me how she had been to the apartment where Blake was now living with his grandmother; there were six people living in a two-bedroom apartment. We both agreed that it would be great if we could get this family a house. Less then ten days later, we had a house (read the story of how this happened in Chapter Four).

Donated guitar autographed by Tim McGraw and Faith Hill

Our goal was to make as many people as possible aware of what we were trying to accomplish and be a part of the event. I reached out to the media: newspaper, television and radio stations across Northeast Ohio. We needed to get donations for goods and services, auction items, and volunteers.

One of those volunteers was June Lambert. I grew up across the street from her. June had been out on the search

Volunteers setting up a tent the night before Blake's Bright Tomorrow

weeks before to look for Jessie, so my dad mentioned how I was trying to put together Blake's Bright Tomorrow. She volunteered to make calls to different businesses to solicit items for our silent auction, and proceeded to work the phones continuously. Ten years before, June had been driving her car when she was hit head-on by a driver who had fallen asleep at the wheel. That driver was killed instantly, and June had every bone in her body from the waist down broken. She was told that she would never walk again. Over time she walked with a cane, but it was hard. Yet there she was out for Blake's Bright Tomorrow, driving to businesses to pick up items, making it into stores, and getting the donations organized. It was amazing.

Now that the word was out, calls from very generous donors came rushing in. The Lebron James Family Foundation stepped up, got involved, and donated an autographed jersey. Within 30 minutes I received two phone calls from travel agencies in Akron, Ohio, wanting to each donate cruises to the Bahamas. The Cleveland Browns, Cleveland Cavaliers and Cleveland Indians all donated items for the auction. A signed Faith Hill/Tim McGraw guitar, which had been won by a family in Cleveland in a national grocery store contest, showed up on my parent's front door with a note saying, "You need this much more than we do." That guitar brought in $1100 at our auction. A man from Raleigh saw the story of what we were doing, and donated a complete collection of mint 1980-2004 Cleveland Indian baseball cards.

The morning of the festival I felt a tap on my shoulder; it was a man who owned a sports memorabilia business. He told me the story about how his mother had been killed when he was 11 years old, and he wanted to help. His donations included five autographed basketball jerseys, one of which was Michael Jordan's. Those jerseys brought in $2,500 that day!

There was a man who owned a promotional product business who called wanting to donate t-shirts for all of the volunteers who were working on the day of the festival. He couldn't afford to pay to have the t-shirts made himself, but took the time to creatively think about how he could raise the money. He sought out other business leaders in the community, and several of those business donated money, and their company names went on the back of the t-shirts. His creativity and thoughtfulness was the reason why all of our volunteers had t-shirts the day of the event. Seeing the look on his face on the day of the event – he was so proud of the part that he played – was priceless.

I often tell the story of the "cookie lady," Nancy Warmus. She wanted to help out in some way, but she was unable to make a financial contribution. So she sought out other ways she could get involved and shared with me her talent of baking. Nancy baked 750 heart-shaped sugar cookies, and iced them all with We Love Blake. Thanks to Nancy's commitment and talent of baking, her cookies brought in $1,000.

These stories show how everyone brought something

Some of the 750 cookies baked by Nancy Warmus

Two hundred pounds of construction paper and markers were donated for children to make cards for Blake.

different to the table and took the time to think about what they do best. Because of their unique contributions and loving hearts, Blake's Bright Tomorrow was off to an amazing start.

The morning of Blake's Bright Tomorrow had arrived, and we began working at 4:00 a.m. There were several of us up before dawn loading up our cars and trucks. As I drove over to the event, my mind was full of the details that needed to come together to make the day a success. The sun was coming up over the horizon at 6:00, and as I pulled into the parking lot, I saw it was already full of volunteers, even though we'd told them that they didn't have to be there until 7:00. The whole community was coming together to make this day a huge success for Blake.

From then on, it was a blur of constant activity by me and the rest of the volunteers. Mennonite churches had put up tents for us to use, and we put out the tables and chairs. Huge professional grills had been donated. Port-a-potties that had been donated were set up. We were blowing up balloons, setting up the silent auction, and getting the food ready in preparation for the event to open.

Soon people began arriving, the music was playing, and the happy sounds of kids having a great time rang through the air. Blake's Corner was a tent where kids could make cards to show their love and support for this little boy. There were pony rides, bouncy castles, places to make candy, magicians, clowns, and face-painters. Hamburgers and hot dogs were grilling, donated slices of pie were going fast, and everywhere people were having a good time. There were over 80 items generously donated for the silent auction, and there were 25 items for the live auction. The weather was beautiful, and the event couldn't have gone better.

Two thousand people came out that day. The day passed quickly, but one event came where time seemed to stop. We brought Blake and his entire family on stage for a very special announcement. This was the moment where we got to surprise them with a house and a playset for the backyard. That moment is one that I will carry with me for a lifetime.

It took teams of people to give this family a fresh beginning, and working for them made us all feel like our lives were better for it.

Why Share a Story?

Working to help Blake has pushed me to want to do more. I want to leave a bigger footprint in this world. Part of that mission is helping inspire others to get involved in effecting change. Sometimes we just don't know where to start, or we allow ourselves to think that others might do a better job at helping than we ever could. Yet if we allow ourselves to think that way, then we risk not seeing the potential in ourselves to effect change.

Don't Change the Channel came to be because I often wonder: What if I had turned the TV to something else? What if I had gone to dinner with friends that night, and tried to put that sad story out of my mind? **We all have *Don't Change the Channel* moments in our lives.** These are times when we have the opportunity to make a difference in someone's life, but don't because:

- Work is too hectic
- I have family responsibilities
- I don't have enough money
- I don't have enough time
- I don't think I can really make a difference
- I'm just one person.

But there are people out there who have the same fears, concerns, and reservations as you. Yet they are out there making a difference every day.

I've had the privilege to talk to people who demonstrate to us all what is possible. Throughout this book there are stories of ordinary people who found that they couldn't go on with their normal day after hearing about an extraordinary need. In life, we tell stories to share with each other who we are, what makes us laugh and cry, and what we find important. These accounts help renew our belief in the goodness of people, and our ability to make change where there is so much despair.

But beyond being inspirational, *Don't Change the Channel* is a book that will empower you with ideas about how you can use your skills and time to make the world a better place. Acts of kindness, both big and small, improve the lives of those around us. Daily acts of kindness are about giving when you see an immediate need in front of you as you go about your day. It could be as simple as seeing a person in the parking lot who is struggling with her groceries, and offering to take the grocery cart back for her. It could be offering a person a spare umbrella if he is standing out in the rain waiting for a bus. It could be holding the door or elevator open for a person who is a few second behind you, and giving that person a warm smile.

> **Acts of kindness, both big and small, improve the lives of those around us.**

Then there are opportunities that require a little bit more of a commitment. This could be volunteering to read weekly to children at a school where the literacy rates are below average. It could mean helping out over a weekend to build a house for Habitat for Humanity. These projects are about seizing the passion for what you feel needs your help the most, and finding a way to make it work with your schedule and abilities.

I've worked on many different projects throughout my life that helped me gain know-how in fundraising and community engagement. Each experience has served as a building block for the next. This knowledge fully prepared me for the moment when I saw Blake's story on TV and wanted to help.

My Story

With my start in life, I had a clear awareness that I was very fortunate. I was adopted at 2 months and 3 days old, perhaps saving me from a life of hardship, and worse, of being unloved. I knew from the start that I had been blessed to have my wonderful parents and sister, a roof over my head, and food on the table. I always felt grateful that I had new back-to-school clothes and supplies every year. I always had the opportunity to participate in Brownies, attend summer camps, and play sports.

I often thought I could have been an orphan, and that is why I grew up knowing that I wanted to help others. I would see commercials on TV about sponsoring kids in Africa or Central America who didn't have enough food or medicine, and those images of starving children would make me cry. I used to take the ads for Save the Children from TV Guide to my dad and ask him to send money to help those kids.

I feel like I'm able to be successful in many things I do now because I had parents who told me I could do anything that I set my mind to. My success is possible because they provided that stability, love, and positive reinforcement.

As I got older, I became more aware that tragedies didn't just happen on the other side of the world – they were happening in my own back yard. There were kids in my own town who had lives that weren't as happy or fun as mine.

I had this keen awareness throughout my teenage years that I could do more with my time than just working after school and hanging out with my friends. In my sophomore year of high school, I heard about the program of Big Brothers, Big Sisters. I decided I really needed to help a little girl who might need some extra attention. I called up the local chapter, found out what I needed to do, and completed the training. Then it was time for me to meet my Little Sister, Dionne. We would go bowling, to the mall, out to dinner, to my high school football games, and over to my family's house for dinner. We talked a lot about school, staying in school, getting good grades and a good education, and going to college, which she did.

Very quickly I found out how invigorating this was for me, and how much joy I provided this little girl a couple times a month. I never wanted to let my little sister down by not showing up, or by being distracted when I did see her. I made sure every outing was fun and special, so that she knew how special she was to me and what an important place she had in the world. I learned that I could make a difference in this girl's life, one afternoon at a time.

When a serious accident occurred my senior year of high school, it showed me that tragedy and heartbreak can happen anywhere and anytime. On January 17, 1991, my dearest friend Kurt was in a terrible accident. Kurt and I have been friends since 4th grade. He is like a brother to me.

That night, Kurt was driving down a road he had traveled a hundred times before. Sometimes, that kind of familiarity can cause trouble. He was on a stretch of the road that had no warning lights or gates for the railroad tracks that ran across it. His radio was on the floor of his car, and we think he leaned down to turn the station, and he never saw the train that was speeding down the tracks towards his car.

The train pushed his car 564 feet down the tracks.

When word got out about the accident at school the next day, we were allowed to go home. Many of the businesses in our small community closed their doors so that everyone could go to his church for a prayer service.

Kurt had dreams of going to the University of Kentucky to be on their golf team. I got "Kentucky blue" ribbon and invited our entire senior class over to my parents' house. Students made ribbons to show support for Kurt and tied them on their cars, which helped unify the school and community. We made posters and signs to show our love and put them around town. Even a billboard sprang up along the side of

Kurt and I on a trip to Walt Disney World

a road. It was a town-wide effort to let Kurt and his family know that we were pulling for him.

Kurt survived. I made a commitment to myself that I would do whatever I could for my friend. I quit my after-school job, and for the next four months I went to the rehab hospital where Kurt was living and relearning many motor skills. Every day after school I would make audiotapes and told him about what happened at school that day. I brought these tapes to the hospital, and his parents would play them for him. After about four weeks of me coming to visit Kurt, and him not recognizing me, I walked into his room and he said, "What's up, Red?" That was his nickname for me. It felt so good for my friend of the past 8 years to remember me.

For 31 years our friendship has never been broken. He reminds me yet again to be grateful for what I have, but he also reminds me that life doesn't have to be complicated to be meaningful and enjoyable. Through him, I learned that acts of daily kindness could make a big difference in a person's life, both for the giver and the receiver.

Assisting Kurt on his journey to recovery and realizing how a community could come together made me seek out other ways that I could make a difference.

From Now On

New stories, events, or chance meetings happen all the time that trigger in me the desire to help as much as I can with as much energy as I can give. I believe I have a calling to connect people with the stories and ideas to spur them on to action. I remain convinced that if everyone looked outside themselves and their daily routine to the world of needs around them, and decided to engage, the world would be a significantly different place.

> **If everyone looked outside themselves and their daily routine to the world of needs around them . . . the world would be a significantly different place.**

As you read, I know that your eyes will open to the opportunities that exist all around you, and you will find within yourself the power to help and succeed. People need to see the world around them with both their eyes and with their hearts. This book will help you to work with your family, your business, your colleagues, and your neighbors to find the time, the passion, and the energy to make a difference.

chaptertwo
chaptertwo
chaptertwo
chaptertwo
chaptertwo
chaptertwo
chaptertwo
chaptertwo
chaptertwo
chaptertwo
chaptertwo

Finding Opportunities To Get Involved

We have become a nation of people who pick up and move every so often, whether it is for new job opportunities, a different type of house, or a better school district. As a result, we aren't so good at making life-long ties anymore. Two hundred years ago, we probably would have stayed in or near our hometowns for our whole lives. Now we don't bat an eyelash at moving across the country for a raise or a promotion. It's hard to stay in touch with friends and family when people don't stay in one neighborhood or town longer than a year or two.

Additionally, technology makes it easy to forget that you need to have actual one-on-one human interactions. After a day spent staring at your blinking cursor on the computer, you may speed through your neighborhood on your way home with your windows rolled up, radio on, and straight into your garage. You may not even think to stop to chat with your neighbor who is walking his dog down the street. Once inside you can eat dinner, return emails in front of the TV, and with some down-time under your belt, be off to bed a few hours later.

When we do go out with friends or colleagues, it has become common to see groups out together at dinner, with all of them looking at their smart-phones instead of actually talking to each other. It's as if the people they are out with aren't significant.

All of this goes against our very nature as humans. Without connection to others, we aren't whole. We forget to look at our surroundings and see that the world is made up of more than our own needs and desires. This mind-set makes it hard to acknowledge and exercise our need and duty to make a difference in our lifetime.

Without connection to others, we aren't whole.

One of the first steps in making a change in our world is opening our eyes up again to the world around us. I'm a big proponent of the power of making face-to-face connections. The human connection is what makes people who we are. When you can look into someone's eyes, you see them smile and laugh. When you shake someone's hand and feel the strength of their grip, you have a connection that is more genuine than what you can ever get virtually. Although technology is important in all of our lives, I think it's vital that we spend time every day getting to know clients, friends, colleagues and neighbors better. You get so much more out of life when you spend time with another person. Our need to connect to people is central to who we are.

A great thing about getting involved in the world around you is the opportunity it gives you to connect to new and interesting people. Fit time for people into your day in some way, shape or form. Think about stopping to talk to that neighbor of yours on the way home and ask how they're doing. Ask the check-out girl at the supermarket if she's had a busy day. Don't give up on real conversations – you might just find something to do or someone to help.

While talking to that neighbor out walking his dog, you

might find out his wife has been ill, and he is having trouble getting all their chores done – like walking the dog. You might realize that you could help and volunteer to walk the dog after work when you get home. That cashier at the grocery store might mention to you, after you take the time to ask how busy she's been, that there has been a huge rush at the store all day. You decide to help her get through her shift and buy her a Starbucks coffee on the way out the door.

Choosing to Get Involved

There are many different ways to get involved in making the world a better place. Look around your everyday life with an open heart to help whomever you might come across on any given day.

With this book, I'd like you to think about what you would like to work on longer term as well. What cause or project that would benefit an individual or community do you want to spend your time and effort on? It could be something that is frequently discussed on the news, or it could be something that is happening down the street. Has a whole community been affected by a big event like an oil spill or floods? Has an uninsured neighbor come down with cancer? Are there more homeless people on the streets because of the economy? Your ability to help depends a lot upon your personal attachment to the cause.

The truth is that many people get pulled into advocating for something because of their surroundings and circumstances. You might have a child on a soccer team, and her coach gets cancer. Your personal connection to that coach and her problem may fuel your desire to help. Perhaps you are a nurse in the Neonatal Intensive Care Unit. Because you work on a daily basis with premature and sick infants, you want to help out with the March of Dimes, a long-established charity that helps prevent premature births, birth defects, and infant mortality. Maybe you play in a band, and you get inspired to help children who can't afford the musical instruments and lessons that you had as a kid and made you who you are today.

You may be on a commuter flight for work, that quickly turns into a nightmare, and then a miracle in survival. I was honored that Dave Sanderson wanted to share his remarkable story with me for this book:

"On January 15, 2009, I was on board the 'Miracle on the Hudson' Flight 1549 aircraft that landed in the Hudson River. All on board survived. I stayed on the plane to check and make sure that everyone had gotten off. I was the last person who was picked out of the water and put onto a ferry. I was in the water for between eight and 10 minutes." The temperature of the Hudson River that January day was just above freezing – 36 degrees, and the air temperature was 20 degrees."

"The ferry that rescued me and some of the other survivors landed on the New Jersey side of the Hudson at a place

Dave Sanderson speaking for a Red Cross event

called Arthur's Landing in Weehauken. Two EMTs met me, along with a man from the Red Cross who had a warming blanket. All three helped take me to the triage room. Because I was in the water so long, I needed to be treated for hypothermia. At the hospital, they had to cut my frozen clothes off of me. It took me five hours to warm up. In the middle of the night, someone from the Red Cross went out to get me some new clothes – I was going to appear on morning television and had nothing to wear but a hospital gown. I don't know how they found me something to wear in the middle of the night, but they found me a tracksuit."

The next day, after telling his survival story to reporters, Dave was anxious to get back to Charlotte. "I was on a plane to come back to Charlotte and finally make it home. It was chaotic on the plane; all the passengers had heard that I was on the plane that had crash-landed, and they all wanted to look at me. When we landed safely in North Carolina, a member of the Red Cross, Pam Justice, was at the airport standing with my family to make sure everybody was o.k."

"My admiration for the Red Cross grew over that 18-hour period. I got to see so many things that they do. They were out there taking care of things for the survivors of that crash."

"Before then, I'd been involved with the Red Cross for a number of years as a blood donor, but I hadn't appreciated the lengths they go to in order to help in these disaster types of situations."

"Pam Justice, who was standing at the airport with my family, was the CEO of the Red Cross in Charlotte. We came to know each other, and she asked me to speak at a fundraising event. I was happy to do it as a way to say thank you to the Red Cross. Melanie Ablehouse of the National Red Cross's Tiffany Circle (a designation for the charity's top donors) had heard me speak at the national convention, and she wanted to have me speak to that group. At that event, I was sitting with a group of women from all over the country, and they raised over 6 million dollars. People were giving me credit for the amount of money that they raised, but I'm just honored that they believed in the importance of hearing my story."

"Now I've spoken at 52 Red Cross events and fundraisers. I am a national spokesperson for disaster services. I've spoken at over 100 other events across the country, and any honorariums that I'm given we send to the local chapter of the Red Cross. I am so impressed at the depth of what they do, which I didn't know about until I needed them that day on the Hudson."

Dave Sanderson felt like he needed to help fundraise for the Red Cross because he personally benefited as a survivor from the disaster relief work that they do. He had been somewhat aware of their mission, but after Flight 1549 he felt the need to get the word out to more people about the great work they do when disaster strikes.

Emotional Appeal versus Pragmatism

Different causes can make an emotional appeal to people. Your family or somebody you know may be confronted with disaster, disease, poverty, mental health disorders, or any number of issues. Because of your personal connection to that problem or need, you have a wish to do something to aid that cause.

One of the reasons I believe I was pulled in by Blake's story was because of my adoption; I could have been someone without parents. I saw Blake as a little boy who had lost both of his parents – one to murder and one to jail. It's scary to think of a child without his parents, and I wanted to be a part of creating a brighter future for him. Whole communities of people got involved with Blake's Bright Tomorrow, as the story of Blake and his mother impacted so many people in so many different ways for so many different reasons.

You could come to a point in your life when there is no emotional reason that one cause over the other is pulling at you, but you feel the desire to have your presence on this Earth make a difference. Bill Gates (and later Melinda Gates) developed what is now known as the Bill and Melinda Gates Foundation out of the desire to help by giving from the fortune made from Microsoft. They took a long time analyzing all the good their money could do for different causes, and they decided that the most benefit that could come out of their investment of money and time was reducing the death rates all over the world by such simple means as providing mosquito tents to prevent malaria, prevent and treat AIDS and tuberculosis. Their analytical approach shows a clear path to people who might want to take a more pragmatic, rather than emotional, approach to solving problems.

Zeroing in on a Cause

Once you have taken the time to think of what you would really like to spend some time and energy on, it's time to do your research. Is there a non-profit or community-based group already in existence helping the cause you are most interested in? If so, do your research about them. Go on the web and read about what their mission is and what they do to make a difference. Find a contact number or an email address, and start talking to the staff to express your interest, ask how their work is being done, and find out how you can best get involved.

For instance, Alzheimer's is a devastating disease that affects many people, and it is going to affect even more and more of our population as the baby boomer generation ages. You might have an interest in it if somebody in your family has succumbed to this illness, or it could be for other myriad reasons. Going to the web, you might notice that there is an Alzheimer's Association for your city. Talk to somebody who works there and find out:

- How can I get involved?
- Can I come to an event?
- Can I see what you guys are doing?
- Can I talk to other people who are involved?

Let's say that the Alzheimer's Association is sponsoring a fundraising walk. That would be a perfect time to immerse yourself in the environment of that association. Talk to people who are involved and the people who are walking, and find out what the group does for people and what the benefits of the organization are for those in need.

If you're interested in volunteering or fundraising for places like schools, hospitals, or libraries, all of these entities will have volunteer coordinators. Talk to that person and find out the different ways that you can help.

Once you have figured out where and how you would like to get involved, talk to your friends and family about volunteering with you. Go to the people in your life and let them know that you're thinking about getting involved. Find out if they have any interest helping as well. If you have a friend who is willing to go with you and is excited to get involved, it helps motivate you with your commitment.

It could be that your partner in community work may have a project that they are passionate about as well, and you can support each other.

Assess Your Strengths

Some people enjoy being told what jobs to do – they like direction. Others like to take charge. Find a role that you feel comfortable in doing that suits your personality. No matter how you fit into an organization, either as a doer or as leader, you are a useful part of the problem-solving puzzle.

When I was organizing Blake's Bright Tomorrow, there was no non-profit or charity in place for me. I had to start organizing this project from scratch, but it was something I felt comfortable doing. People were calling and asking to help when the word got out about what I was organizing, but they didn't know how to help. I was able to give them specific ideas about how they could assist the cause, and they could choose what they wanted to do from that list.

This leadership role is vital in crisis situations among individuals as well. When someone dies, often the most common way of reaching out is to ask the bereaved family, "If there's anything I can do – let me know." The majority of families won't take you up on this because they are in shock and going through a terrible time. They are not in a place where they can think of things for you to do. Their lives have been turned upside down. Take the burden off the family to come up with something that will help. Decide what to do and see how you can work it into their schedule, or just get it done. Buy some groceries for them, with some basic foods as well as some treats. Mow their lawn so they don't have to worry about it. Hire a maid service for a month to come and clean the family's house.

As you think about ways to get involved, think about what you are good at. Are you good at making phone calls? Are you good with people? Are you good at crafts and decorating? Are you a good writer?

> **As you think about ways to get involved, think about what you are good at.**

You may be a whiz at technology, and you notice a school's website is terribly unorganized and could be so much more useful. You can volunteer to help. You may be a terrific baker, and volunteering to bake cookies for the monthly lunch that your church brings to the homeless shelter would be easy and fun for you. You may love to play basketball, and your local sports recreation center down the road has just had its budget cut and no longer has coaches – you could step in and coach the kids.

How Much Time Can You Commit?

At different stages in life, you have different amounts of time that you can commit to helping others. Those who are parents of young children and are also sons and daughters of seniors who may be experiencing health problems are often called "The Sandwich Generation." They're taking care of both the younger and older generations, which can be extremely time-consuming. However, if you are a parent and would still like to do something, think of an activity or place that will allow you to participate with your children. If one of your parents is in a nursing home, see what you can do to put a smile on someone's face after visiting your parent. You're already spending a number of hours a week there, but wouldn't it be nice if you could visit somebody who doesn't have someone to visit them?

Think about how much time, realistically, you have to spend on volunteer time. Could you do an hour a week, or do you have time for only an hour a month? Can you do five hours a week? Be honest with yourself, and don't commit to more than you can reasonably do.

My mom is a retired teacher; one of the things that she is involved with is volunteering for a program called Ohio Reads. This program is for kids who might be a little behind in their reading skills. Mom's strength is that she is a great teacher. Her passion is education. Her time level is such that she can commit to a weekly time with these children. She wants to retain that connection with the schools and kids and make a difference.

Kenna is at a different stage of life, attending university. I met her through the Make-A-Wish Foundation. Here is Kenna's story:

"When I was ten years old, I was diagnosed with acute myelogenous leukemia. I was told that I had a 43% chance to survive, and I would need an adult protocol of chemotherapy since this was not a disease normally diagnosed in children. For the next seven months, I was in and out of the hospital receiving chemotherapy, as well as treatments for the many infections I developed due to my low blood counts. I was approached by someone from the Make-A-Wish foundation a few months after my diagnosis. I was told that I could receive a wish, and I needed to think about what I would want."

"I wished to go to Hawaii and was surprised on live television when my wish was granted. My family and I went in June of 2002. It was the best vacation I have ever been on. I remember that the people at the car rental office saw "Make-A-Wish" on our paperwork, so they upgraded us to a convertible. Can you imagine driving around in a convertible in Hawaii for a week? It was awesome! While in Hawaii I swam with dolphins, went snorkeling, went to a luau and rode horses to Captain Cook's monument. The trip was so much more that I could have ever dreamed of."

"Throughout my treatment I met many wonderful kids who were also battling cancer. One of my dear friends also received a Make-A-Wish. I was there when he was surprised with his wish, and the look of joy on his face was almost like getting my wish granted again. I love that I was able to see the power of Make-A-Wish in a child's life and experience it myself. This organization really does make dreams come true, and I am so thankful that I can share my story and be involved with Make-A-Wish in any way."

"I am now a sophomore at North Carolina State University, majoring in biological sciences and Spanish and adopting a minor in non-profit studies. I hope to attend Physician Assistant school upon graduation from NC State, and I would love to work in a pediatric oncology clinic. I will continue volunteering for Make-A-Wish and keep them close to me throughout my life because I can honestly say my Make-A-Wish was one of the best experiences of my life. I will never forget it."

It's interesting to see in Kenna's story that not only does she want to help other kids who get cancer, but she is still involved in Make-A-Wish activities because she has experienced first-hand what life-enhancing work they do. So her work and her volunteer activities follow her passion and experience – what a great combination!

You've learned in this chapter some of what motivates people to get involved in specific causes. Everybody's reason will be different, but the end result is the same – volunteers are making change in this world for the better. By connecting to the world outside their own lives, they are bringing everybody a better world.

5 things you can do today
5 things you can do today
5 things you can do today
5 things you can do today
5 things you can do today
5 things you can do today
5 things you can do today
5 things you can do today
5 things you can do today
5 things you can do today

5 things you can do today

Spotlight: Neighborhoods are a place where we want to feel comfortable and safe. Part of getting to that place involves knowing your neighbors, and making the area around you beautiful.

Here are some ideas to do today to make your neighborhood a better place:

1 Check in with a neighbor today and see how they're doing.
2 Find out who is in charge of your community watch program – what's happening in your neighborhood.
3 Pick up someone's trash can.
4 Clean up your community day – beautify, pull weeds, or paint mailboxes.
5 Organize a street get-together.

chapterthree
chapterthree
chapterthree
chapterthree
chapterthree
chapterthree
chapterthree
chapterthree
chapterthree
chapterthree
chapterthree

Talking To Everyone
about Your Cause

Everyone has to start somewhere with a cause, and that somewhere usually involves a phone and a list of people to call. That list is going to grow, change and develop into the lifeline for your project. When you are ready to start talking about your project and your cause, it's time to start letting everybody know about it.

Make a list of people you want to contact. It could include:
• Neighbors
• Business contacts
• Former colleagues
• Friends
• Relatives
• Service people you use – your hairdresser, your grocery store, your pharmacy, your plumber, etc.
• Local media (when it makes sense)

Utilize your connections. **Everyone is great at something**. Use your talent and then find the others around you who are good at different things. When I get excited about something, I call everyone that's in my world, and before you know it, I've got all these great types of people involved. Your checklist of helpers will fill up faster than you think.

Here's the easiest part of your whole project. Get a

folder, and write the project name up top. Stick in lots of pieces of paper.

For every person you call, write his or her name somewhere in that folder. Keep this with you at all times so you have names and numbers handy. You never know what you'll be in the middle of when somebody calls you back, or you have an idea in your head that you need to jot down before you forget it.

Blake's Bright Tomorrow started with a pen and some scribble in my folder. While other people may love nothing more than assembling a great spreadsheet on Excel, I don't work that way. Use what works best for you.

As the event grew and took on a life of its own, I ended up having a folder for every part of the project. I had folders for media, donations, house information, volunteers, food and beverage and so forth.

Everybody is different when it comes to getting in touch with people. Some of us are shy, and some of us spend all day on the phone. I love nothing better than to pick up the phone and call people. Other people can't stand the phone. They will do anything possible to *not* use it. My mom is one of those people. When I was working on Blake's project, my mom would have rather scrubbed the floor with a toothbrush than picked up the phone and asked people for a donation. She wasn't going to do that – that was my job. But once she started talking with friends and neighbors and other contacts in the community, it got easier. Mom found the work she was doing so exciting that talking about it to the waiter at a restaurant wasn't hard, and neither was asking for a gift card to add to the fundraiser!

So for phone avoiders, it's time to realize that the phone is an asset when you're working on a great project. You need to get on the phone and call around to let people know what you are taking on. Contact those friends, clients, colleagues, and neighbors. They might send you to other people who may help, be able to brainstorm with you, and help in so many ways you won't believe it.

Tips for Talking on the Phone

Keep the message simple. You've got ten seconds to make a first impression and pitch your story. People don't have time for you to "um" and "ahem" while you remember what you want to say. Get to the point. You need a who, what, when, where and why of what's happening. Practice, practice, practice before calling your contacts. You have a limited amount of time to capture their attention and get them on board as a helper to your cause. If you are afraid you're going to get your words mixed up, write a script. Practice that script so that it does not sound like you're reading off a page.

Call potential donors and volunteers back if you leave a message and don't get a return call. People want to see and hear your enthusiasm for the cause, and that will be demonstrated by your persistence and determination.

> **People want to see and hear your enthusiasm for the cause.**

The first couple of rejections you get might be hard to take. You might even feel after a couple that you want to shut the whole thing down, saying, "I stink at this," and go back to your regularly scheduled activities. You've got to be persistent. People should be open to helping out with a great cause, especially if they see the drive, passion and determination to succeed in you. If you all share a common goal, to make this person or family's life better, you will have a good success rate.

When it comes to helping, you never know if someone is going to say yes until you ask. If you didn't put the time in to make those calls, how would you have gotten to those two or three yeses?

It can be hard to determine ahead of time what cause is going to strike a chord with someone. The manager of your local grocery store might have grown up in a family where his dad lost his job. He knows what it's like to not have enough food on the table, so he might respond if you're raising money for the family down the street whose breadwinner just got laid off. That store manager may give you a gift card because he can see himself in that situation.

Other people may need to know who else is getting involved in the cause. They want to know if this is a reputable cause that you are raising money for; they may be concerned that their donation might not go where it's supposed to go. Reassure the skeptics by letting them know who else is on board – which businesses are going to help, which people around town have offered assistance, which newspaper reporter already knows the details of the event. This will help with the credibility of your venture. I have also found that having a letter with contact information or an email address ready to give out was useful for many people, as they liked to have something in writing.

Other Ways of Connecting with People

Of course you don't always have to contact people by phone. So many of us are good at going out and meeting with friends and colleagues, and many people find that face-to-face contact really helps stimulate their thinking.

I have hundreds of clients that I talk to on a regular basis. Every conversation I had during the months that I was helping out with Blake's project, whether it was at lunch, on the phone, or at a meeting, we ended up talking about this project. Everybody brought some insight or a new contact to the table. For instance, we needed water for 2,000 people for the fundraising festival in Ohio. I was talking to a friend of mine who owns a bottled water company. He heard what I was doing and got in touch with a gentleman in Cincinnati who was in the same industry. That person ended up donating the water for 2,000 people for that event. Had I not talked with my friend, none of that would have happened.

When people know that what you're calling about has to do with helping someone else, and they hear the enthusiasm in your voice, you will get people contacting you. A girlfriend of mine in Charlotte worked for Sprint and had a friend that worked for a food company in Cleveland. She knew we needed hamburgers and hot dogs, and that person ended up giving us hamburgers and hot dogs to feed 2,000 people.

It's amazing how networking can work.

Connecting with people can take time, and you need to decide what the smartest way is to use your time. Once you've got people on board, group emails can be a great way to let people know what's happening. Those emails can be forwarded to more family, friends, and colleagues at the touch of the button.

Getting to an Answer

Talking to everybody about your cause will not only lead to more people to network with, but it might also help you zero in on your best strategy for success. For instance, if you're trying to fund something at your child's school, a series of phone calls might lead you to come up with the great idea and the people to help you execute that idea.

Another scenario that might happen is that you think you might have an excellent idea: you want to rent a place and have a big party there, but it turns out they won't negotiate their rates down for a charitable fundraiser. A friend might tell you that golf courses are closed on Mondays, and that is a great time to hold a charity fundraiser because you won't be disturbing any of the golf club's regular members.

Courtney

This story of an amazing little girl helps illustrate the power of making calls and asking people for donations.

Ten years ago, I was working for a local radio station, and they were hosting their annual fundraising campaign for the Children's Miracle Network. That Saturday, I was out running errands and listening to the station when I heard this woman being interviewed. She was mother to a three-year-old little girl named Courtney. During her interview, the mom was talking about how Courtney had already had 104 surgeries. Even though I had arrived at the store, I didn't get out of the car. I couldn't turn away from this woman's story. I thought, "What little body can handle 104 surgeries? How lucky I am to have my health, and I'm out shopping for my new house."

Courtney's mother told the interviewer that her little girl likes Mickey Mouse.

I decided I wanted to send Courtney to Walt Disney World.

On Monday I went to Mann Travel, a local travel agency in Charlotte, North Carolina. I told them the story about Courtney, and the owners were so moved they gave me airline tickets for the entire family of five.

I used to work at Walt Disney World, and there's this amazing place close by called "Give Kids the World." Give Kids The World is a non-profit organization that exists only to fulfill the wishes of all children with life-threatening illnesses and their families from around the world to experience a memorable, joyful, cost-free visit to the Central Florida attractions. I used to volunteer there on Wednesday nights. That is the night that parents are able to have a night out and do something fun for themselves. It's an amazing place, and everybody there is happy. Kids are even able to get ice cream 24 hours a day!

I got in touch with Give Kids the World, and before you know it, we had an all-inclusive week arranged for this little girl and her family, complete with food, rooms and tickets to go to many of the area's attractions. As an extra Christmas surprise, I decided to go to the Disney store to buy some Christmas stockings and fill them full of goodies.

Through Children's Miracle Network, I called the family and told them I worked at the station, had heard their story, and wanted to come and meet them. When I got there, I told them, "You're going to Disney!" The look on their faces was of complete disbelief - they thought I was crazy. When they realized I was really telling them the truth, they were so thrilled. They had a great time and were able to have fun as a family.

About a year later, Courtney died. I'm so glad this family has those wonderful memories of their vacation together.

Getting the Word Out

There are different ways of reaching out to people to let them know about your event or cause. I'll discuss newspapers, radio/TV, social networking, and grass-roots movements that will help with both big and small events.

I'll use Blake's Bright Tomorrow as an example because as an event, it got a lot of attention. This was incredibly helpful as I organized it in so little time.

As soon as I had a location, time and date for the festival for Blake's Bright Tomorrow, I knew I had to get the word out about the event so I could start getting volunteers, donations, and people to come to the festival. I called all of the media: television, radio, and newspapers in the cities surrounding where the event would take place in Ohio - Canton, Akron, and Cleveland. In many cases in busy newsrooms, you have to make your case quickly and succinctly.

Because the media had extensively covered the case of

We received local and national media attention for Blake's Bright Tomorrow.

Jessie's disappearance and murder, the reporters I spoke to were immediately familiar with the cause I was supporting. Everybody I talked with agreed to get the word out on their broadcasts and in the newspapers. I had 100% participation. Radio and TV stations had our information up on their websites. I even called some of the national media – The Today Show, CNN, Good Morning America, and so forth. I wanted the whole country to know what Jessie Davis's hometown was doing for her son.

I had needed the media to get involved, especially because I was arranging the event mostly from Charlotte, North Carolina – 500 miles away. (I didn't get to Ohio until 3 days before the event.) I phoned in radio interviews in the week leading up to the event to say that we need your help, your support, and your presence at the event. Once the stuff started hitting the newspaper – my phone was ringing all day!

So many people who had been on the search for Jessie felt a bond to the family's loss, and they really wanted to be involved in the fundraiser. Business leaders wanted to be involved.

At first I only had basic information, but as I got donations and participation, I was able to share some of the exciting news about what we would have at the festival. It gave the cause validity. As the donations came in, the excitement around the event grew, and people were able to understand that this was going to be an amazing day.

I told the story about what we were trying to do to anyone in my world, whether they were friends, coworkers, clients or the media. The more people you touch, the more people get the word out.

Having a website for the event and cause was crucial for me to be able to refer people to. A website company volunteered to create a site and worked three straight days setting it up. Several people worked around the clock, and they did that all for free. Our website, www.BlakesBrightTomorrow. com, allowed everyone to see more information on what we were doing and how they could donate money.

We also designed a flyer with all the information about the event to encourage people to attend. We got in touch with a printer in my hometown, and we asked if they would be willing to donate their printing services. They agreed and printed out 1,000 flyers for free. Volunteers then went and put the flyers up around town in grocery stores, barber shops, the windows of people's businesses, and post offices. These flyers were everywhere. They also ran the flyer in the local newspapers.

I had a lot of friends who I had contacted, and they were making tons of phone-calls – a gigantic phone tree extended all over the country. Because everyone has their own network of people – they were trying to utilize folks from their world to let people know what they were working on and trying to get the word out. People were making phone calls asking for gift cards and certificates from businesses, inviting people to the event, asking for media exposure, and so forth. We were making sure that people were making connections wherever they were.

I was on the phone non-stop. Within three weeks I had used 10,000 minutes on my cell phone. My phone bill was $1,000. I called AT&T to explain and see whether they would help me out. The customer service representative I spoke with was in Kansas City, and she was familiar with Jessie's story from the news. They credited my phone bill $700.

I was getting almost daily emails from somebody somewhere to check in, ask how things were going, and how else could they help. One of the most memorable donations that we received was from an 80-year-old woman in San Diego, CA, who sent in $15. In the memo of the check she wrote, "With love." I called this woman to thank her – her phone number was on the check. She had worked in real estate her whole life and was retired, and she said, "I don't have a lot to give, but I wanted to send something to help this little boy." All those 15 dollars add up, and I was so touched that a woman as far away as San Diego had reached out to Blake's cause.

Working with people in the community who helped run the town was essential. I called the local police and fire stations, as well as the sheriff's office, to let them all know about the event. We needed help with crowd control, traffic, and security. Plus, kids always love seeing a fire truck. They all jumped in and were eager and willing to participate. Several local churches got involved as well. They baked goods for our event, in addition to donating chairs, tables, plates, and napkins.

As you can see, for this one cause we tried to cover as many bases as we could.

Social networking is now an essential tool that helps disseminate information about events and donations, can give videos and links to websites, help find volunteers and more. Had Facebook and Twitter been around in 2007, they would have been great tools to utilize connections on top of connections.

5 things you can do today
5 things you can do today
5 things you can do today
5 things you can do today
5 things you can do today
5 things you can do today

5 things you can do today

Spotlight on Hunger: Many people in the US today, and countless people abroad, do not have enough food on their plates everyday and often go to bed hungry. Here are some ideas where you can help:

1 Make a "Girls' Night Out" event, and volunteer together to work in a soup kitchen or a homeless shelter.

2 Surprise the person in front of you at the grocery store and buy their groceries.

3 At your child's next birthday party, instead of presents, have everyone bring canned goods. After the party, take a field trip to the local food bank to show your child what a difference their party has made to help feed the hungry.

4 Designate a portion of your child's allowance to go to buying food for your local food bank. Take your kids to the grocery store with you and let them pick out the food they want to buy.

5 Sign up with your local public school system and become a lunch buddy in an underprivileged area. Enjoy lunchtime with a child who may be in need of positive reinforcement, and help them make healthy food choices.

chapterfour
chapterfour
chapterfour
chapterfour
chapterfour
chapterfour
chapterfour
chapterfour
chapterfour
chapterfour
chapterfour

Businesses and the Community

Part of getting involved in a cause is letting everybody know about what you are doing. That includes your colleagues. After all, many of us spend more time with work colleagues than our own families.

Have you ever correlated the success of the company you work for with the amount of volunteer work and giving it lends to the community? What gives a corporation a good reputation in the eyes of the public? What makes an employee happy to be a part of a company besides a good management team and good corporate benefits?

> **Have you ever correlated the success of the company you work for with the amount of volunteer work and giving it lends to the community?**

I think that the overall success of a company and the happiness of employees could be markedly improved if it had a community engagement program. After all, businesses operate and work out of a community, and its employees reside in the area. Doesn't it make sense that a business should have a program that operates to ensure that it is an active and engaged part of the community?

Every company, big or small, with one office or multiple offices, five employees or five thousand, industrial or service-driven, should have programs in place that encourage the business and employees to take time to get involved with the community.

A business should be more than just getting work done and then going home. Shouldn't that relationship offer more than a paycheck?

Fortune Magazine picks its annual "100 Best Companies to Work For" list, and part of the criteria on which they are judged include: credibility (communication to employees), respect (opportunities and benefits), fairness (compensation, diversity), and pride/camaraderie (philanthropy, celebrations). Employees who feel that their company is not credible or philanthropic might have low energy levels and lower morale. Their creative talents may be untapped in many areas. Workers may not know people they work with on a significant level. People may be counting down the time left until the weekend.

Employee retention is higher when employees feel like their company is making a difference in the world. When you have a management team that empowers people to come up with projects or ideas to make a difference, then you feel like you have a voice in many projects and are part of a bigger solution. Employees may have better relationships with management if they have a different rapport then just delivering work-related materials. When you start getting involved in your community, you start to see people more as humans and not just as coworkers. You hear their stories, and they hear yours. If someone's son is playing on a football team, your whole office gets excited for that family when they win the big game.

You see a transformation with people where work is not just a job but is more of a work family; you're in an environment where your business is involved with your community. While a business cannot be all things to all people, it will be a much more positive place if it has a community engagement program.

Founding a Community Engagement Program

What does having a community engagement program mean? This should be defined by each company interested in starting one.

If you are an employee, and your business doesn't have any good works sanctioned by the company, it's time to take action. Talk to co-workers, and gauge their interest in starting a project. Get the buy-in from them. Pick their brains about what they would like to work on. Then, go to management with two or three good ideas. Ask for their support as you put something like this together.

For instance, you might be so busy that you can't take time for lunch, and you normally eat a sandwich at your desk. However, you and your co-workers want to start going to serve lunch at a shelter once a month, and you need permission to be gone that extra 30 minutes. Take that idea to management - see whether they'll agree to it, or maybe you can negotiate a way to take time that's agreeable to all parties.

Start up a committee with people from all parts of your company to consider:

Is this a program that gives a defined contribution to an organization each year, gives volunteer hours, or both?

Is this a program that aligns itself with one community partner, or does it allow employees to find their own places to volunteer?

How should volunteer hours be treated by management?

Are they earned, awarded, or rewarded?

There are many different ways that businesses can be socially responsible. Here are a few suggestions:

- Have a beneficiary if you recycle/donate used or out-of-date office supplies and equipment
- Volunteer time
- Donate a percentage of profits
- Hold fundraisers
- Mentor students/grads/unemployed
- Sponsor local teams/schools
- Inaugurate scholarship programs
- Create awareness for causes to your customers and clients.

An office may be involved haphazardly in any one of these efforts, but wouldn't it be amazing if each business made a concerted effort to form a cohesive policy?

An ordinary office might see the efforts of a few people trying to get support for their cause on a one-one basis. Some parents sell Girl Scout cookies for their daughter's troop, and that may benefit the individual troop. Maybe somebody in the office gets a diagnosis of breast cancer, and an informal team from the office decides to do a walk in support of that colleague in order to raise money for research. While these actions are all doing good, none of these solo efforts are working with the company in an official capacity to assist in these endeavors.

For instance, in the case of the employee who had breast cancer, what if the situation had been brought to the business's community engagement group, and they decided that this was a cause that the business as a whole would like to get behind? They could hold a kick-off gathering to gain members for the team, and incentivize the walker with the highest donations with the offer of a restaurant gift card. The company could donate t-shirts with the corporate logo on it for Walk Day. There could be a "Wear Jeans to Work" day, and everybody who wore jeans could donate $5 in honor of

the team's walk. The company newsletter that goes out exter-
nally could feature the work that the company was doing to
find a cure, and customers and clients could be encouraged
to give. Think about the differences that each one of these
actions could make to the success of this team of supportive
co-workers, and then you can start to see what could happen
at your own company.

Finding the Right Business Fit

There are many ways to align your business with causes
and endeavors. Some companies might want to have a strategic way of looking at what they do and how their services,
products, and expertise can best help benefit the community.
For instance, if you work for a company that makes paper,
then perhaps you can donate paper to your local school system. If you are part of a group of accountants, perhaps a non-
profit needs pro-bono accounting help.

Trent Haston and the team at Andrew Roby decided to
sit down and come up with a community engagement program. Trent is the Vice President of his family-owned construction business. This is the 60th anniversary of their business, and the 3rd generation is now involved in running the
company.

"Our company values our customers and employees. We
have always treated our employees well, and we sponsor Little League teams as coaches and supporters. But in 2008, we
decided that in order to be the company we needed to be, we
needed to hang our hat on something bigger. We asked ourselves: how do we take what we do with our skills, vendors,
subcontractors and customers, and get the biggest return for
our resources and our time? We didn't know how or what
that was going to be, but we wanted to get a sign. We cal-
culated the amount of time we could give and the resources
we had available. We interviewed charities and asked them

This group from Andrew Roby raised over $40,000 for the Leukemia & Lymphoma Society.

to make us a presentation about what they do and how we could help. One of the charities we invited was the Leukemia and Lymphoma Society because one of our 24-year-old workers had lymphoma, a form of leukemia. Since our company had a personal connection, we decided to go with LLS."

"Our philosophy when looking at working with the charities is that we want to do real good for the community – how is working with a charity going to benefit our employees and our standing in the community? If we gave LLS a check for between $3,000 and $5,000, we would also love to have our involvement with the charity and have the charity carry our brand. We wanted to raise $5,000 and get our vendors and subcontractors to sponsor a tournament. We made shirts, created signage, and sent letters out to customers and clients. We would prime the first $5,000. We have 20 associates and spent 1,000 man-hours between July and September trying to make it work. Our goal was to net $20,000. We ended up raising $30,000."

"Last year, we increased our net goal to $40,000 in the worst recession ever, and we made it."

"Our company held the biggest fundraiser for 2008. The Leukemia and Lymphoma Society made me the corporate chairman for the Charlotte chapter's 'Light the Night,' which is their fundraising walk. We put our name out there in the community as a company who helps. The fundraising experience I gained led to me being recruited for a position on the local board of The Make-a-Wish foundation, which I happily accepted."

"We post our philanthropy missions on our website: we are 'pursuing a vision of leaving Charlotte a healthier, happier and more beautiful place.'"

"We post our philanthropy missions on our website."

"If you want to lead and want people to give, you've got to lead and give. Somebody stopped me the other day near a house we were building. He said, 'I think you all are doing great work in the community.' To hear that makes me appreciate how our philanthropy really brings value to our business. I'm a big believer in paying forward."

"Our employees love getting involved. I've always paid people for the hours they work, and I don't want to overburden them with extra work, but our employees want to contribute their time unpaid. It tells a manager a lot about employees who want to volunteer."

> **It tells a manager a lot about employees who want to volunteer.**

Having a policy and action plan in place at your business is good for the workers, and it is good for the reputation of the company. Customers and clients may choose to do business with you over others because of the work your company does in the community.

Ideas for Companies

Many large corporations bring in famous speakers to help motivate their employees. In addition to that, why not recruit speakers from local non-profits to come in and let people know what work they're doing in the community? It will help educate your workforce, as well as give people an opportunity to align themselves with a charity that might need volunteers. Local hospitals, Red Cross, schools, and community services programs could all come in on community days.

> **Why not recruit speakers from local non-profits to come in to our business and let people know what work they're doing in the community?**

Alternately, you could have a day once a quarter where employees talk about the things that they've been involved with, as well as the impact it's made on them. That would help give the limelight to a special employee, and it would give their charitable work a broader platform on that day.

Instead of having a team-building day at a retreat, why not actually build something like a house for Habitat for Humanity house together? Imagine the sense of accomplishment that everyone on the team could feel, as well as the

The staff at King's Kitchen

enjoyment you could get out of seeing the quietest woman in your office show her skills off as an expert carpenter. Everybody would be seen in a new light away from the office. Similar ideas for a day away would be volunteering at a local soup kitchen, having a sing-along at a nursing home, or hosting a Dress for Success event for female employees to find a good home for their gently used business clothes.

Sometimes group volunteering efforts lead to whole new endeavors. The work that restaurateur Jim Noble is doing with his latest venture, King's Kitchen, shows how one workgroup found that volunteering a couple of days together a year wasn't enough. Chef Noble currently has five restaurants in North Carolina, with plans for more restaurant launches next year.

King's Kitchen is a non-profit restaurant with the mission to feed the homeless. Everyone in there – from the employees who work there to the patrons who are enjoying its well-received food - is making a difference in their community. Here is Jim's story.

"According to the Bible, a good business is not there to take for itself, but to benefit and be involved with the community. It can be very easy for a business to be single-minded and short-sighted about its profitability. A business should be part of the community, not taking from it."

"Homelessness and hunger exist in Charlotte. We should not think of it as a problem, but as an issue we need to deal with because we live in this community and need to be a part of the solution. There are many great things happening in Charlotte, but we can't ignore the bad."

"We have been in the restaurant business for 27 years, and our ministry began 12 years ago. For many years, we have been serving the homeless during Thanksgiving and the holidays at all four of our restaurants, but we felt like we weren't quite doing enough. I believe we're only limited by what we're willing to imagine or believe. If we take the lid off our pre-conceived notions, we can see what we need to see in order to make changes."

"My wife Karen suggested that we ought to have a restaurant that feeds the homeless as its purpose. She had seen a documentary on Café Reconcile, part of a diocese ministry down in New Orleans. They work with at-risk folks who'd been through rehab and had been incarcerated, to teach life skills and job training. Profits go to feed the poor."

"Seeing what they had done inspired us, and we started working on it two and a half years ago. Our employees have all wanted to help. People want to do good, but sometimes they don't know how. Two years ago we had our first fundraiser for it, and now the restaurant is up and running, open for lunch and dinner. As we get further along, our at-risk trainees will make up 30 or 40% of the staff. The program will be a 50-week process, with training in leadership, restaurant skills, and social skills. The restaurant must be profitable to feed the poor, so it's in everyone's interests to be well-received and liked by the community."

"My businesses and I have only been "above the fold" in the newspaper two times. Both times, it had to do with my non-profit work. That is great exposure for everything that I do."

> **"My business and I have only been 'above the fold' in the newspaper two times. Both times it had to do with my non-profit work."**

Make the Most out of Opportunities for Kindness

Opportunities for acts of kindness often fall into the laps of those businesses who work directly with the community, such as operators of store-front businesses and service companies. There are easily recognized methods of going the extra mile to form a good relationship with the public to ensure customer loyalty, such as having a generous return policy if you're a store, replacing ice cream dropped just outside the front door if you're an ice cream shop, or working late to get the problem fixed if you're in a service business. These measures all ensure customer loyalty.

But what happens when good customer service goes hand-in-hand with charity?

Dave Sanderson, who we talked about in Chapter 2 recounting his "Miracle on the Hudson" USAirways flight, also had a good story of an act of kindness given to him by a retailer. It ended up benefiting the Red Cross, whom he works so hard to raise money for.

"After my belongings were fished out of the Hudson River a while after the flight, I saw that my Mont Blanc pen and pencil set had come out of the river ruined. I went to the Mont Blanc store, and they were nice enough to replace them for free. My visit to their store actually ended up in their newsletter. They were so tickled at the response they got that they decided to sponsor a private book party at the store for *Brace for Impact*, the book about the flight. All proceeds of the sale went to the Red Cross. We made over $800 in 90 minutes for the Red Cross that day, and I believe their reputation has benefited from this act of kindness. I'll certainly be a lifelong user of their products!"

Think how many customers Mont Blanc got into their store that day to visit with Dave and hear about his experiences and the book. They also got to see first-hand the good work that Mont Blanc was doing, and see their products. Mont Blanc went above and beyond good customer service and garnered themselves a new reputation.

Redefining Your Business's Mission Statement

Does your business's mission statement say anything about how you work with the community? When Andrew Roby Construction decided to get more involved in the community and good works, they put it up on their website as part of their philosophy.

In my own work life, I practice what I preach when it comes to marrying the business that I am in with community engagement. I am the Executive Director of a business networking club. Six years ago, we revamped how we were going to run the business. We are a networking group, but we make it perfectly clear to the people involved with us that this group is half business, half community involvement. We have two scholarship fundraisers that donate over $25,000 each year to our local school system.

This is a group where everyone feels part of a family and consciously makes a difference every day in Charlotte.

The flagship event for our club is a monthly breakfast regularly attended by 350 people. Once a year we bring in

Public Service Scholarship fundraiser held in honor of two fallen police officers

a motivational speaker that every age can benefit from and enjoy. We open the breakfast up to members' kids of all ages – we've had kids from age 6 to their early 20s, and it's a very powerful day. Seeing these kids interact with new people, shaking hands, being interactive, and getting to spend time with their parents – it's impactful for everyone. We've had great feedback about what that day means to the parents and the children, and how their kids never forget that special day.

One very special breakfast we did was in response to a community tragedy. On April 1, 2007, police officers Sean Clark, 34, and Jeff Shelton, 35, were killed on duty, execution-style, here in Charlotte. Both men were married, and Officer Clark's wife was 8 months' pregnant and had another child. Out of respect, and because I felt like it was the right thing to do, I went to the visitation – I stood for five hours with many of my fellow Charlotteans. But there were others who had come from all over the country. One thing that stuck out to me was that people were coming from work, with UPS and FedEx drivers still in their uniforms.

Days later, there was a processional to their funerals and final resting places. All along one of our major thoroughfares where the processional traveled, flags were flying and little kids were standing with their parents on the side of the road. In all the years I've lived in Charlotte, I have never seen the public react to an event with so much emotion. There was also, understandably, so much anger that these two young lives were cut short in senseless violence. I decided that I wanted to have a breakfast to bring our community together to honor the fallen officers. We turned it into a fundraiser to go towards the scholarship fund for the children of public safety departments, which was established by the Rotary Club of Charlotte after 9/11.

As demonstrated in Chapter 3, I utilized my list of contacts to try and make this a successful event. I am friends with the CEO of the Charlotte Regional Visitors Authority, who runs our convention center in Charlotte. I told him I wanted to do a breakfast to bring the entire community together to honor these two police officers and donate money to the scholarship fund. He loved the idea and donated the convention center. Next, I was able to engage Chief Richard Picciotto, the highest-ranking firefighter to survive 9/11, to come out and speak at our breakfast.

We sold out the convention center with 1,800 people that morning. A lot of businesses bought extra seats so that they could have public safety workers as guests. We had 600 police, fire, paramedic, and sheriff's department workers. We raised $30,000 in one morning.

Because I wanted those who could not come to the breakfast to feel like they were involved in the celebration of these officers' legacy, I went to the local Fox affiliate here in Charlotte. After many discussions, Fox decided to cover the event live from 5 a.m. to 10 a.m., and from 7 a.m. to 10 a.m. there were no commercial breaks. The morning was filled with stories of courage in the name of public safety – from New York to here in Charlotte.

PSA announcements on Fox ran to promote the event. The major newspapers covered it. Many mass emails went out. I spoke at different Rotary Club events so that they could be involved as well. There was a call for people to make donations on television and on our website.

After the event, I received a hand-written letter from an FBI agent, thanking the breakfast club for holding the event and telling us how special it was to public safety workers. His name is Jerry Senatore. Since that day, he has been involved in our breakfast club. Now he's fighting non-Hodgkins lymphoma, and everybody in the club is now raising money for his bone-marrow transplant at Duke University.

Because of the paradigm shift our breakfast club made six years ago, we have tripled our size, have a renewal rate of over 95% with our members, and we have built the reputation as the best group in the city. This shows how community engagement work can actually help grow a business.

> **Community engagement work can help grow a business.**

A Culture of Caring

This culture of caring and fellowship that we created in this group meant that the members became absolutely instrumental in helping out with Blake's Bright Tomorrow. Although this work was for a state 500 miles away for people they never met, over 100 businesses in Charlotte got involved. Thousands of dollars were raised to go towards funding for the house and Blake's college fund. The message that came out of this involvement was this: here are two communities in two different states brought together because it was the right thing to do. I believe it stands as a great example for business groups everywhere. The community engagement work you do doesn't just have to be in your own community – you might be touched by something several states away, but you can still work together to make a difference.

One group that was invaluable in helping Blake's Bright Tomorrow was the Home Builders Association of Portage and Summit County, Ohio, which is a non-profit association. They received a letter from journalist Ann Kagarise, who was instrumental in helping Blake's Bright Tomorrow. She was a reporter covering the case from the beginning, and we worked together to try and figure out a way that Blake and his family could have better living accommodations. How this group of home-builders dealt with this request was remarkable, and shows how innovatively they were thinking. It also helped turn their association culture into one of caring that is still rewarding them years later.

Len Huddleston was President of the Board at the time. Here is what he remembers about how his group was asked to get involved with Blake's Bright Tomorrow. "We received a letter that asked, 'Is there anything you all can do to help Blake's family get into a home?' As a non-profit organization, we don't have the funds to donate a house. So I thought that a lot of banks were taking over houses – and I wondered whether we had any bank members that have foreclosed homes that they'd like to donate? We had an answer within 48 hours that Countrywide would give the Davises a house. Immediately we started putting committees together and called suppliers and contractors. They donated labor and materials. 120 people volunteered – no one said: 'No.' It was overwhelming the amount of help that we were able to assemble."

Len Huddleston talking to the media at Blake's Bright Tomorrow.

"The time that this all came together was the start of the downturn in the economy for homebuilders. Even so, the participation we had was unbelievable. It all came so easily. Seventy percent of the homes where I'm paying people to show up and work on a house don't go as smoothly. When they were volunteering for the Davis house, people were showing on time and doing what they said they were going to do. The attitude of the volunteers was, 'We were more than happy to even be asked.' The people who worked on the house felt good inside, and it gave them a sense of fulfillment. They gave with their hearts and didn't think twice. Nobody in there was doing it for the recognition. These opportunities don't present themselves too often – so many of us didn't want to look the other way."

"People may say to those of us in our company, 'I know

you from somewhere, and I don't know where it's from.' Sometimes it's from what we did for Blake's family. Everybody I know that helped us is still in business, even in this tough economy."

"Everybody I know that helped us is still in business, even in this tough economy."

"For me personally, this felt like exactly what I needed. I was going through a divorce, my father had died, and the economy was going downhill. I don't know how I would have gotten through that period in my life without staying busy and helping others."

The work I do on a daily basis with my networking group coming up with ways to help the community is incredibly fulfilling. When your company starts up its Community Engagement Program, I know that it will help change the culture, success, and the level of pride that all employees feel about the place where they spend so much of their time.

5 things you can do today
5 things you can do today
5 things you can do today
5 things you can do today
5 things you can do today
5 things you can do today
5 things you can do today
5 things you can do today
5 things you can do today
5 things you can do today

5 things you can do today

Spotlight on Unemployment: With so many people out of work in the current economy, there are many opportunities to help give someone in need of a job. Here are some ideas you can do today:

1 Go to your local library or job center and volunteer to help people write their resumes.

2 Buy a bag of groceries for your unemployed friend or neighbor.

3 Take gas gift cards or bus passes down to the unemployment center.

4 Dress for Success or Goodwill – Drop off business clothes that you no longer need to help others look great for their interviews.

5 Invite an unemployed person to a networking event with friends and colleagues – you never know whom you might meet.

chapterfive
chapterfive
chapterfive
chapterfive
chapterfive
chapterfive
chapterfive
chapterfive
chapterfive
chapterfive
chapterfive
chapterfive

Kids Making a Difference

Imagine what the world would look like if we could harness the boundless energies of every child to become involved in fundraising, mission work, or volunteering? There are approximately 70 million people under the age of 18 in America. Children have a willingness to help and a belief that anything is possible. The world would be a much better place if more children were involved in these activities.

Getting kids involved in charity work is an excellent way of starting a lifetime of good works, and it is great for their self-esteem. Kids who volunteer serve as excellent role models for other children. Volunteering also helps create a good work ethic, teaches discipline, gives a broader perspective on the world outside your door, and teaches how to follow through. If parents and children volunteer together, it's great time spent outside the house that will open up new areas of communication and togetherness!

Children are born with an innate sense of wanting to help. If you are around babies who play together, you will find them helping each other – offering toys to play with, or giving hugs or kisses (of course, you will also find them fighting, but we'll overlook that part of growing up!). This thoughtfulness and sensitivity to the needs of others, no matter how big or small, needs to be encouraged from their earliest interactions with others, and then it should be broadened as they are more able to engage with the larger world.

Children are born with an innate sense of wanting to help.

If you happen to observe a well-run pre-school, you will find children working together to do projects big and small. They will pass crayons back and forth, share a glue stick, and get one another tissues during cold and flu season. They wait patiently in line to go places, and they will let one another know if they are doing something that is hurting somebody. Clean-up time is fun and active, with absolutely everybody participating and taking responsibility for cleaning up toys and art supplies. Teachers and assistants nurture this kind of behavior with praise and excitement over all the good that is being done. If somebody gets hurt, then there might be multiple messages of sympathy and empathy, as well as commentary from other children about what happened the other day when *they* got hurt.

The most influential people in children's lives are their parents. I'm fascinated by how the influence of parents can affect a child's inclination to help one way or the other. Great parents model behavior to teach life skills, manners, kindness, and on and on. Many of the people in this book became the caring folks they are today due to their parents demonstrating the essential message that we are all responsible for each other.

My friend Paige Twer has a 5-year-old daughter who wanted to help sick little kids. Here is what Paige has to say about what happened, and how her family life has changed as a result.

"What started out as a simple request, for a 5-year-old to collect some change while holding her first-ever lemonade stand, sparked a charitable wave our family could never have

*AnneLeigh and sister Juliann, 5 and 3, at their lemonade
stand for Make-a-Wish*

seen coming. Our 5-year-old asked if she could put together
a lemonade stand, the kind she had seen other kids do many
times on our neighborhood corners. This was not a surprise.
AnneLeigh loves to work on new projects. The surprise was
that she didn't want to make money to buy the latest toy or
her most recent "want." Instead, she was looking at a desperate, national "need" that even some adults have not been able
to open up their eyes to, especially as we are all just trying to
stay afloat in these tough times."

"From the backseat, AnneLeigh said, 'Momma, I want to
have a lemonade stand and yard sale and give all the money
to sick kids.' We could have said something like, 'What a
nice idea, maybe we can get to that some time,' or we could
have explained to her that we really didn't have time to do

anything right now. Instead, we went right home and started researching organizations that could be potential beneficiaries. After listening to her options, AnneLeigh decided the Make-A-Wish Foundation was the perfect fit. Her dad asked her why she chose Make-A-Wish and she said, 'Because I know if I was as sick as those kids, I'd want someone to grant me my wish.' She decided she wanted to raise $199 so that she could send as many Wish Kids to Disney World as possible. Little could any of us imagine that young, naive goal would soon be realized and even shattered!"

"AnneLeigh immediately got to work by holding conference calls, touring the local Make-A-Wish offices for tips and supplies, and enlisting bakers and area business donors along the way. My husband and I gathered the details and information, and then we simply sent out the call for support through email. Although we were not surprised that friends and family answered that call by offering up items for sale, baked goods and cash donations, the extent of their generosity blew us away! Even before the weekend event kicked off, AnneLeigh had already collected $439. The first afternoon, she collected an additional $442. We wrapped up Saturday morning with another $483. That short weekend event totaled $1,364 to donate to Wish Kids."

"Amazingly, though, it did not end there. We continued to get phone calls and emails asking if it was too late to help. Of course, we agreed to extend our donation period. In the end, AnneLeigh's 'First Annual Lemonade Stand and Yard Sale' raised **$3,882!** While we are thoroughly in awe of the donations that AnneLeigh's event brought in, we are even more thrilled with this wave of generosity we feel. We know that we have a very special, huge-hearted little girl. In addition, I think this experience shows so much more about the quality of people who surround us. Friends and neighbors, young and old, stopped by to drop off goodies, bring an extra table, or just to lend a hand and offer support. The checks, well wishes, and prayers poured in from North and South Carolina, Illinois, Indiana, Kentucky, Florida, Arizona and even as far away as England!"

"AnneLeigh had the idea, the plan, made the contacts, and gave us our marching orders. Michael, her 3-year-old sister, Juliann, and I just obeyed what God had put in her young heart. As I type through my tears, I feel so grateful that she is mine to call 'daughter.' My 5-year-old philanthropist may have just fulfilled her own wish of sending Wish Kids to Disney World. This is her next wish — that other kids, even as young as she is, will hold events like hers in Charlotte and around the country so that even more Wish Kids will get to smile. I am certain this is just the first of many charitable ventures AnneLeigh will have in her life."

Paige talks a lot about what is age-appropriate for kids who want to get into giving and volunteering. Because many of their family friends have kids that are older, it's hard for them to grasp that they need to wait for certain things. If her children see a need, they want to know if there is a way they can help. They think Mommy and Daddy can do anything – and they get upset when they find out we can't help everyone. Paige has to remind AnneLeigh that it's o.k. to be a kid.

However, while Paige and her husband are busy teaching their girls about what they can and cannot do, the girls are raising their own awareness about what they can do. As Paige and her children were leaving a parking lot, a homeless man was holding up a sign: "Hungry. Need food. Please help." They had just come from a restaurant, and they had a box of leftovers. The girls made Paige do a u-turn in order to give that man their leftover food.

Another time, AnneLeigh got carried away. When they were volunteering as a family for Room at the Inn at their church, her daughter started pulling the princess sheets right off her bed. She wanted to give her bedding to a little girl who might be homeless. Paige had to remind her that it's not o.k. to give everything that they have, and they have to take care of themselves first before they are able to take care of someone else. AnneLeigh was convinced that she should clear out her room and get money for it, and she wanted to give 100% of it away. Paige feels it's her job to help Anna Leigh find her correct balance and realize it's o.k. to have something for herself.

When Paige took her children to Walt Disney World, they got to see children at Give Kids the World who were very sick. They saw a 17-year-old in a wheelchair who couldn't speak and had never walked. Paige's girls would ask questions about these children, and they didn't shush them. Instead, she explained to them how they were ill. Children shouldn't feel badly about their questions. It's only as an adult, after years of experience, that you recognize clearly when something or someone is different.

Paige says, "I expect my children to look the homeless in the eye. I do not want them to be sheltered or to have insecurity interacting with people who are different. Everybody needs to feel like a human being and get a look of love from a fellow human."

There are so many lessons from AnneLeigh's story:
* Dream big
* Get the word out
* Keep balanced
* Look at life the way your children do
* Look everyone in the eye.

Saturdays at the Y

My own family was constantly giving and doing something in the community when I was growing up. My mom taught for 30 years in the public school system. My dad, Charlie Snyder, is 69, and he is still very active both in business and in the community. Dad has boundless energy. When my sister and I were kids, you name it, and my dad was doing it. When he wasn't volunteering at our church or with his Rotary Club, he was also a member of different boards and worked with our school system. Whatever activities my sister and I were involved with, he made sure he participated at some level with the organization.

One of the major impressions on me was the involvement my family had with the Hattie Larlham Foundation. My parents had a son who died very young before I was born. One way my dad was able to keep Johnny's memory alive, and help do the same for other families who had lost a child, was to be on the board of that foundation, where Johnny lived for the last few weeks of his life.

"When we knew that we had to put Johnny in a place where they could give him more specialized care than we could give him, we met Mrs. Larlham. Not only was she a fantastic person, but we pretty much fell in love with the place. In 1972, Johnny died, and thereafter we started making donations to the Hattie Larlham Foundation in Johnny's honor. Mrs. Larlham's son had moved to a place right near my office, and when I ran into him one day, he said to me: 'You know, we're looking for people on the board. I think you would make a good board member.' I got a call from another member of the board, who also asked me if I would serve. I've been on the board ever since. I look at it as a way to serve. I'm not a person who can give thousands of dollars, but I can volunteer and help out with fundraisers."

"I'm not a person who can give thousands of dollars, but I can volunteer."

I know this service means so much to my dad.

More volunteer work evolved as my sister and I were growing up. My sister was involved in competitive gymnastics for 15 years. Dad ended up in the kitchen and put together all the food for the meets. I'll let him tell the story.

"The main reason I got involved in the kitchen was that the gymnastics meets ran all day, but Kristin competed for only about two minutes of that time. It was just something to do to occupy my time, and I enjoy cooking. I would cook chickens for the chicken sandwiches the night before and make sloppy joes. For the big meets and the district meets, there would be between 350–400 girls. I would make sandwiches and have sausage and egg casseroles for breakfast. During the regular season, each parent was supposed to bring something for the kitchen."

My father makes it seem like no big deal, but I don't know many people who would come home on a Friday night after a long week at the office and happily start roasting chickens and making the filling for sloppy joes. Kicking back with a beer and falling asleep in front of a game wasn't my dad's method of operating.

Saturdays mornings, my dad would load up the car before it was even light outside. He would work in the kitchen, making and selling food all day. The only breaks he would take would be to watch my sister's routines. When the meet was over, he would often be the last one to leave. He would do all the cleaning, letting other parents leave so they could be with their kids. These were 12-15 hour days, when Dad could have been doing any number of other things with his weekend time.

Dad was approached because of his years of service to the YMCA to start one up in our hometown. "Our town didn't have a YMCA, but there was one about five or six miles away. I had been on a couple of committees with the YMCA, and they had given me some awards, Now they were talking about putting a YMCA in our community. Four or five of us sat down and decided it was something we wanted to do. It probably took about eight years from the time we talked about it to when we made it happen. We finally formed a YMCA, but we didn't have a building. We had meetings and events at schools and senior centers, but what we really needed was our own building. I happened to be the President of the board at the time those decisions were made. We broke ground and had a number of really big fundraisers – but they have never been my cup of tea. I could work them, but I was not the type of person who could go to the money people – I had problems doing that. We were told by the national YMCA group that for a town of our size, we could expect 2,200 members, so when we were planning the YMCA building, we built it for 3,000. The day we opened up we had over 3,000 members. Now we have over 7,500, and it's been open for five years. We are now in the process of breaking ground for an addition."

I'm so proud that my dad helped found a YMCA in our hometown, and as you can see, it's very popular!

I grew up doing so many activities at the YMCA; I was involved in summer camps and athletic teams. I knew what the YMCA meant to me when I was growing up, and I had seen my dad's involvement with it. So when I moved to Charlotte, I immediately became a YMCA member. I am now proud to sit on the Dowd YMCA board here, and have gotten very involved in the YMCA programs throughout the Charlotte community.

Volunteering and Family Time

When you grow up in the environment I did, you see your parent making the casseroles, and you help with the plates, napkins, and cups; it's all about learning how to help others. You learn how to be a part of the team, and see how every member's job is important. This gives you a good work ethic because you see what does and does not happen if you are not there to help – how others can struggle if there are not enough hands to do all that needs to be done.

I feel very strongly that while playtime is important for kids, so is doing something constructive with your time. When I was in the kitchen at those gymnastics meets, I got to spend time with my dad, who I didn't get to see much of during the week because of him being at work and me at school. It's great to have activities that you can do together at night or on the weekends, and it's making an impact on the community.

Many parents are focused on leaving work at a certain time in order to get their kids to baseball practice, soccer, or piano lessons. When your kids are doing activities you may be driving them, but you're not really participating with them. They're the ones out on the field, and you're sitting on the sidelines. It might be easy to see that if your children are good at a sport or in the arts it's going to help them later in life. But think about what volunteering can do for them as well. It's going to look equally impressive, if not more so, that your child is a fully engaged and vital part of an organization trying to make the world a better place. When you're doing work with people you love, you're all getting dirty together serving meals at a soup kitchen, cleaning up the local park, or making beds at a homeless shelter – parents are no longer on the sidelines.

It might be easy to see that if your children are good at a sport or in the arts it's going to help them later in life. But think about what volunteering can do for them . . .

If you recognize that volunteering as a family has not been a huge part of your life, it's time to have a family meeting. It is important to recognize that many children are not in what used to be considered a traditional family of a mom, a dad, and a brother or sister. Family time can also be for blended families, single-parent families, foster-care families, or families in which the grandmother is raising the children. Every type of family can benefit from doing volunteer work together. Sit down and ask your kids what they would like to get involved with to help. Help them think through the causes – whether they are personal or general. Go on the internet with them and look at different websites for the works that have them.

As a father as well as a member of the clergy, Chris Payne is passionate about emphasizing to children the need to help in the community. As a child, his parents took him out. "One of my earliest memories is after church on Sundays my parents would pack us up in the station wagon, and we would pick up food trays at a hospital. We would deliver these trays to widows who lived in a difficult part of town, and we would sit there and talk with them. This is one of the first exposures to poverty I had growing up. This was possibly the only meal that these women might get, and it could have been the only conversation they might have that week. I still remember the sights and smells. My parents were adamant about us all going together. Even though I remember not wanting to be there, it was an amazing experience to take white suburban kids into the inner city and see the worlds collide."

"This kind of experience teaches you that you don't have to be the smartest person or do things on a grand scale to make a difference. It teaches kids that your life is more than getting good grades and going to the right school, marrying the right person, and making a lot of money. Bob Buford, in his book *Half Time,* talks about shifting your life from pursuing success to pursuing significance. There's nothing wrong with success, but it's got to be more than success for success' sakes. Cultivate that heart in your kids and people around you."

"One of the things we talk about with our congregation is modeling a life of service for your kids. One of the most important things you can do is to invite them on an adventure of serving other people. This helps kids see their parents as people who are making a difference – whether at their jobs, in schools, or wherever it might be. Parents will be leaving a legacy of the importance of helping other people. The world is an adventure if you treat it that way. My wife and I took a trip to Africa on a mission trip. When we came back, we spent the last month telling them what we did, saw, and experienced. It gives kids a larger world-view: the world is so much bigger than their own backyard, and there's a lot of need. The world needs your gift, and it needs your engagement."

Model a life of service for your kids.

When disasters strike, oftentimes it's kids who will shake their parents down for ways to get involved. Kids are not so numbed by the tragedies around them that they feel like they cannot help. They are deeply affected by images of suffering from natural and man-made disasters, famine, and war. They haven't yet seen that these things happen far too often, nor do they worry about the difference that just one person can do. It is the job of parents to encourage, rather than discourage, the efforts of a child. Don't be the one to tell them they can't help, because they surely can. Make this a learning opportunity for a child to give back. If they see positive results from a lemonade stand, a bake sale, or a barbeque, it will light a fire in them to see their energies and efforts result in a solid accomplishment.

Building Work Ethics

One of the benefits of children volunteering is that it helps to build good work ethics. Wherever the place is that you want to volunteer with – you have made a choice to get involved. When you get involved, other people depend on you. Your time on that project matters, and you will typically get back whatever it is that you get involved with. There might be meetings that you have to attend, or an event might need prep-work. Certain tasks will be assigned to you.

When you step up at an early age, you can demonstrate how important it is to show up on time to a meeting. If you have been assigned or volunteered to make phone calls for donations, that money will not come in unless you make the effort.

Let's say your son says that he wants to visit people at a nursing home to brighten their days. Hopefully he will envision the consequences of what might happen if you let other people down. If you say you'll be there on Tuesdays, you have to follow through. When you start to be responsible at a young age, you develop habits that instill discipline in you. This will carry over to when you get older and need to study for exams. Those good grades might lead to scholarships, and they may even help you to land your first job. They are all building blocks on top of one another – they are teaching you how to be responsible.

Children will also find out what can happen if the job that they have taken on is too big for them. For instance, your child may have beautiful handwriting and wants to volunteer to address envelopes for a big gala that a local charity is throwing. If guests don't get their invitations, nobody will come, and no money will be raised. It's a crucial job. However, it may quickly be discovered that addressing 1,000 envelopes takes a lot more time than your daughter anticipated, and with all her other commitments, she realizes she can't get her job done in a timely manner. It's time to problem-solve. Help your daughter come to a solution. Perhaps she can have a pizza party, and after her friends help her address 50 envelopes each, they can break out the pizza.

Middle and High School

Now that you're older, it's time to push yourself out of your comfort zone. You can learn a lot about yourself, as well as discover what you like and don't like doing. The different opportunities that you allow yourself to experience will help guide you in your future path.

You'll read in Chapter 9 how *Don't Change the Channel* went into the classroom to help children think about how they have helped other people, or how people have helped them. Reflecting on those experiences made the children realize what an important thing it is to go out of your way to help somebody. A few of the middle school students wrote the following stories about how they were inspired to make a difference.

"A year ago my neighbor was diagnosed with breast cancer. I made pink heart earrings and gave them out and people gave donations. I raised $700 for the Susan G. Komen Foundation in her honor. Every Monday she had her chemotherapy, and all of the donors wore their earrings every Monday. About seven months ago she died."

Another story reads:

"My church was doing something called serving evangelism, and for about 3 weeks we collected groceries to give to people that didn't have any. My group went to a trailer park, and we knocked on this lady's door, and she had 2 young kids. We explained to her what we were doing, and she actually invited us into her house. We told her what church we went to and why we were handing out groceries. She began to tell us her life story. She explained that the kids were not hers; they were her grandchildren, and their parents had been killed in a car accident. She then told us that she was in the process of peeling her very last potato. We gave her the groceries and continued to return to her house with groceries every few weeks. She ended up coming to our church. We also helped her financially and started a trust fund for the kids. She was able to get back on her feet, get a job, and put the kids in daycare."

These stories are so incredibly powerful, and you can feel the pride that the children have in writing their good work down.

Wouldn't it be great if every high school had a day where

all kinds of charities showed up, told the kids about what they do, and shared how kids could get involved? I think this would spark a real upswing in volunteerism. I know some high schools are now requiring service hours, and this would be a great way to make a match between cause and student.

Another great thing to do as a student is to intern. This may not seem like it iss volunteer work, but it actually is. There are many companies out there who are struggling to make ends meet with fewer employees. Although these businesses are for-profit, they still feed families, give them shelter, and move the economy along. When I was in high school I thought I wanted to be a sports broadcaster, so I wanted to start interning at radio and TV stations. It was hard getting internships the summer before my junior year. I picked up the phone and started calling local radio stations – back then they wouldn't take you unless you could get college credit for your work. I convinced the station to let me come and work for free. That experience was valuable to them – I helped them with many little tasks that needed doing, and it led me to find out that I *didn't* want to be a sports broadcaster!

As a teenager, it's so easy to be selfish and just worry about yourself. You can spend your summer vacations playing video games, texting your friends, perusing Facebook, and relaxing before the next school year arrives. But this is such a good time to be out there helping, pushing yourself to find things you like to do beyond your normal routine.

As you get older, you can see the consequences of certain decisions and choices you have made– it all starts in childhood. It is the responsibility of adults to expose children to that message.

Self-Esteem

Self-esteem is lacking in so many kids for many reasons. They may not be getting positive reinforcement at home, they may be hanging out with friends who are not supportive, or they may have peer pressure telling them what they do, say, look, or feel is not normal. Self-esteem is so important to who you are – you have a better chance at understanding what's right and wrong, and making the right choices, when you know that what you're feeling is right for you.

When you got involved in positive activities and are around positive people, it is bound to boost your self-esteem. An 8th grader sent in this story to *Don't Change the Channel's* website.

"One day someone offered me a smoke. My friend Chris, who I had known all of my life, took it and smashed in on the ground and said, 'That's bad for you.' That's a good friend."

There are a couple of lessons in that story. One is that Chris had excellent self-esteem, and he knew that his friend shouldn't be smoking, no matter who offered him a cigarette. Another is that his friend stood up for him, which showed him that his friend cared enough to make that bold, decisive move.

You have to have good self-esteem to make good choices; you want to stand up for your friend, and for yourself, and hear the voice in your head that smoking is bad for you. It's a teaching moment for the other person – it's o.k. to stand up for what is right.

I had two girlfriends growing up named Gina and Jennifer, and we did everything together. We made a pact that we were not going to smoke marijuana, even though several of our friends did. It was common at some of the parties that we attended for marijuana to be available, but we made that pact in our sophomore year of high school. When there are three people making a pledge, you're connected and you have a better chance at sticking to that choice. You know that you're not the only one who is not going to do it. Once we told them at parties, 'We're weed-free. We're not going to judge you for the choices we make, but we're not going to do it,' teenagers didn't pressure us. Not only did they not pressure us, but they still wanted to be our friends, and hang out with us.

Anything is Possible

One of my favorite stories this year was one I saw this past January on Oprah. It was a weekend when I was at home sick, and I was not getting off the couch. I decided to catch up on my recorded shows on DVR. The Oprah show had on this boy who really captivated my attention. His story had me up off the couch, trying to find out more information about this young man and his good work. Since then I've been telling everybody about him.

Aaron and Eric Ware were twins who did everything together. Aaron said of his brother, "He could find something good about any situation. He could just totally lift your spirits." Tragedy struck when Eric was diagnosed with brain cancer, and he died when he was 10. Depressed and feeling alone in the world without his twin by his side in life, Aaron and his mother sought help from his pediatrician. They tried conventional fixes, but it was not until his pediatrician, Dr. Marilyn Corder, tried to get him engaged in something he liked to do, that a smile came onto his face. "Baking," he said, and the light turned on in his eyes. "Then that's what we're going to do," said Aaron's pediatrician. She prescribed starting up a business, and she funded him $20 on the spot to get his business started. "I'll be your first investor," she said.

"It gave me something to do, and we did everything together, so having nothing to do is like not living So I started baking and I just love it," said Aaron.[1] Now he is the founder of a business called Doughjangles: Sweets by Aaron. The

---

Interview CBS News: "A Baking Prescription," March 7, 2009, www.cbsnews.com/video/watch/?id=4835166n

whole family helps in getting cookies out to the neighborhood and around the country. Proceeds from sales benefit the charities that helped his brother and his family get through the heart-wrenching days of his brother's illness.

According to the Doughjangles' website, Aaron recently attending baking camp, where he learned to bake: crème brulee, brownies, cheesecake, and puff pastry. Aaron hopes to one day attend culinary school and make a career out of his hobby.

I often find myself thinking about this boy and his family, and I carry him around in my heart. I pray for him and his family. I have been trying to think about how to help him expand his business and sell more cookies, and I hope I get to meet him one day. There are days I go back and watch that show just to get inspiration from his story. I really applaud the pediatrician who took the extra time to give Aaron a cause and a purpose that rallied his spirits.

Self-esteem is so vital to the well-being of children, and tapping into what made Aaron feel good was his salvation. For Aaron, seeing his business turn profits into cash for charities to help other children must make him feel really good.

The stories that came from these children are so inspiring. I know that if more kids got involved, this world would be even more incredible than it is now.

5 things you can do today
5 things you can do today
5 things you can do today
5 things you can do today
5 things you can do today
5 things you can do today
5 things you can do today
5 things you can do today
5 things you can do today
5 things you can do today

5 things you can do today

Getting Kids Involved (Plus 16 more)

This list of ideas came from Randall Middle School in Lithia, FL. The kids were so enthusiastic about sharing their ideas, they came up with many more than five. I couldn't leave out any of their great thoughts!

1 Buy someone lunch or give them lunch money.

2 Have extra supplies so that you can give them out if other students don't have supplies.

3 Hold the door for people, even if you don't know them or don't like them.

4 If there is another student that you don't know, look them in the eye, smile and say hello.

5 Compliment 2-3 new people everyday.

Bonus Ideas

6 Invite someone you don't know to sit with you at lunch.

7 Have a conversation with someone you normally wouldn't.

8 Post random sticky notes in the bathroom and around school with positive comments, like "You have a nice smile" or "You are beautiful."

9 Smile at everyone you see.

10 If someone looks upset, ask if they'd like to talk.

11 Treat everyone with kindness and respect.

12 If someone drops their things, help them pick them up.

13 Help someone with their work if they don't understand or need help.

14 If you messed up, make sure to say you're sorry.

15 Try to listen more instead of always talking or just waiting to talk.

16 Stick up for someone if they are getting bullied.

17 Start a gratitude journal with your friends.

18 Talk to the new kid.

19 Be kind, even when you don't want to be kind.

20 Don't gossip or talk about people behind their backs; don't let your friends gossip either.

21 If someone is alone, invite them to sit with you or walk with you.

chaptersix
chaptersix
chaptersix
chaptersix
chaptersix
chaptersix
chaptersix
chaptersix
chaptersix
chaptersix
chaptersix

Under-Utilized Workers

Imagine what the world would be like if all those who are seeking employment would get involved in community work. Because of our troubled economy, unemployment has grown, and those who are seeking jobs right after college are in a bind as positions have dried up. Women, who stayed at home with their children when they were young and then decide to go back to work, are finding it hard to re-enter the work force. Retired folks have voluntarily left the workforce because they worked long and hard, saved well, and are reaping the fruits of their labors.

All of these people have an amazing opportunity to utilize themselves in the community. Their un-employment, or under-employment, means that they have, like it or not, something many others do not: <u>time</u>. They might have said it many times over the course of their days, whether spent studying or at work: "I wish I had time to do more to help." This moment in time, whether chosen or not, is a great chance to get involved in some fulfilling volunteer work. The benefits will be returned in so many different ways.

Recent College Graduates

The headlines in newspapers across the country declared this to be the toughest job market in a generation for new college graduates. The Class of 2010, and probably that of 2011, will be looking back enviously on the days when graduates could pick and choose from a host of companies offering meaningful careers. But now, graduates have months and months of waiting even for interviews to open up.

This can be an incredibly discouraging and worrying time, as student loan debts are piled high. Twenty-somethings long to move out of their parents' houses and get places of their own.

While I can't help with the economy, I can share with you what has worked for me and for others: make volunteering and interning part of your job search. Intern as much as you can – at places that relate to what you want to be doing. Offer up your skills and your time in the community – hospitals, food pantries, schools, and non-profits. Think about how you would like to help out during this time when you are not working. Not only will you be giving much needed free labor, but you'll also be able to tell future employers how you spent your time in such a valuable way.

Make volunteering and interning part of your job search.

You never know whom you're going to meet when you're out in the world giving. You might meet a person who has a lead on a job opening, or you might meet a person who has a job you'd never thought of, but sounds incredibly fun. Meeting new people expands your horizons and opens unexpected doors.

If you're still on campus and worried about getting a job after graduation, take advantage of what's going on at your college or university. There are lots of opportunities to get involved in different programs and activities on campus. If you happen to get involved with the planning of a charitable event, this is terrific experience in event planning, marketing, organization, networking, and cross-promoting. A great example is Jessie Miller's story on the charity work that she did while at Duke. An incredibly bright girl, Jessie had the goal after college of getting into a veterinary medicine program, which had very few open slots for the thousands of people who applied.

"While I was on campus, I volunteered at the Durham Animal Shelter and the Lemur Center at Duke University. At the animal shelter, I walked dogs that otherwise would just be in their cages, and I helped puppies learn how to play well with others. It was a lot of fun. At the Lemur Center, I volunteered with the veterinarians, and I helped out with research, observations, and surgery. I was also a part of the Pet-I-Care club, a Duke student community service group that raises awareness on campus and in the community about the companion animal population in Durham. They also educate the public on the importance of proper animal care."

"The vet program I was applying to at NC State required 100 hours of animal contact and 400 hours of vet experience. All of the recommendations that I got for my veterinary school applications came from vets I volunteered with. Volunteering and networking were essential to me for getting accepted, and I am still in contact with all the vets who I worked with. People are happy and appreciative that you put your time in to help."

Volunteering is going to make you more marketable because it makes you well-rounded, and it shows you have a compassionate side and care about the community. It might give you that edge over the thousands of other kids who are competing for the same graduate placements or jobs. There might be 100 of you for one job, but it is very appealing to hiring managers to see that a person has done internships and non-profit work. That could get your foot in the door.

Hiring managers know that if you're connected to your community that you care about others. You're more likely to be engaged in the welfare of their colleagues and clients. Your experience could mean that you'll be the one who spearheads new projects and brings fresh energy and skills. You may serve as an inspiration to other people who have been there for several years.

Some of the benefits of being part of this age group are that you have a lot of energy and are unlikely to have family commitments that would prevent you from being actively involved. You have more free time on your hands than what a mother or father of young children would have. If you are young, volunteer for some of the more physically demanding jobs out there, such as building houses for Habitat for Humanity.

Many non-profit organizations have young professional groups. To encourage the future philanthropy of those under 35, these groups combine social activities with a charitable overtone. Usually for a small monetary donation, they get involved in a lot of projects.

Tara Masten, 26, helped to found a young professional group, The Starlight Society, with others at the Levine Children's Hospital. "The group was started over a year ago by Matt McLanahan, a young man whose father is a doctor at the hospital. He knew that there was this age group who wanted to get involved in the hospital, but they didn't yet have the financial abilities to give in a significant way. The hospital already had a group known as the Dream Catchers, which is for people in their mid-30s and up."

"The main initiative of the Starlight Society is to get people involved in the hospital who just graduated up to the age of 35. The financial obligation is low: just $10/month

Tara Masten and fellow volunteers for the Starlight Society at Levine Children's Hospital

for 2 years. With that money they do a variety of events, both social and fundraising. They have had events where they hope to grow the group: happy hours, watching minor league baseball games, and bowling outings. But the best part is that once you're involved, there are volunteer opportunities. To be a volunteer at the hospital usually takes hours and hours of training. For those with full-time jobs, however, it's difficult to be able to undertake this kind of training. With the Starlight Society, you can be involved in a significant way without the time commitment."

"The money we raise goes to a stage in the children's hospital. Kids can come down for different activities, and we also can bring in entertainment acts. We had a beach bash, and we organized beach games, crafts, and music. We got together and made these cute invitations for the patients, and their families were invited. We also have magicians, musical groups, speakers, and more themed activity afternoons. The mission of this group is that as you grow more financially sound, hopefully you'll be invested in the children's hospital."

Tara was out of work for five months, but the networking skills she developed volunteering were incredibly useful in a difficult environment for the unemployed. "During that time, if there was an event, I was at it. I met new people, and a lot of times what we talked about was my charitable work. To strangers, when you can describe the cause and why you do work for it, you really come across as a far more credible person. In this economic climate it is so important to be out there. If somebody invites you out to something – just go. Learn to adapt. Volunteering has made me a valuable person."

Stay at Home Moms/On-Ramping

A number of women, and more and more men, are "off-ramping" out of the work force when their children are born. They decide to stay at home to be with their children when they are little.

While some never return to the workforce, many do want to go back to earning that valuable paycheck. The gap in years when they weren't employed in the business world may seem difficult to explain. Of course, we all know that being a parent is the toughest job in the world that has no end on the time clock. But future employers want to see whether you were involved in any way outside the home.

This gap in formal job descriptions on your resume would be the place to put in the volunteer work that you've done. Enumerate the skills that you learned while working in the community.

Elizabeth Kurtz had long worked in the corporate world in property management, and then she stopped working full-time when her two little boys were born. As her boys got older, she started looking for opportunities to re-enter the workforce and had just begun sending her resume out.

The time of Elizabeth's job search happened to coincide with a volunteer opportunity at church that she had decided to participate in. A program called WISH (Workforce Initiative for Supportive Housing), run by Crisis Assistance Ministry, needed teams of trained volunteers to work with families called Hope teams. The idea is that the volunteers would work one-on-one with families in need of supportive folks to model middle class behaviors for them – kind of like a Big Brothers/Big Sisters program. This program works with the poor to help break the cycle of poverty and to prevent families from becoming homeless.

"I thought the program was a great way to volunteer and utilize my professional skills. The church was providing between five and ten Hope teams, and I signed up to start the training program. In between then and the time when the training came around, a job was posted for a housing coordinator with Crisis Assistance Ministry. I sent in my application for that job. When training for the Hope program, I met the volunteer coordinator for Crisis Assistance Ministry and told her how I had applied for that job. She and the director of the program talked the next day, and the director called me to come in and talk about the job."

Elizabeth thought this was a great way to spend time if she was not working. "Whatever you like doing and you're good at, find charities that could use your skills. Let it play out and see if your volunteer experience can lead to full-time employment. In my case, I didn't really think that volunteering would end up leading to a job, but it worked out great."

See if your volunteer experience can lead to full-time employment.

"I think a lot of people have the misconception that there are not volunteer jobs that would be stimulating intellectually.

But there is so much out there that you can use your brain for – websites that need building, phone banks that need manning. Crisis Assistance Ministry uses a lot of volunteers to help for our Emergency Financial Assistance program. We had 296 people in line this morning, and 30% of the staff working with them is there on a volunteer basis. They are essential in helping us work with families to discuss their needs, fill out paperwork, and so much more."

WISH funding comes from churches, private individuals, property management companies and others. "That's how we fund salaries for volunteer managers. Rent subsidies come from city. Those who are getting a housing subsidy meet with a social worker once a week about setting goals, financial management, and ways to increase earning power."

"My new job description is that I manage the relationship with properties and our families, and I go out and recruit new housing developments to work with us. My job provides an additional layer of support for both the families and the property managers. If my client is delinquent, the property managers can call me directly and know that I'll work to make sure that isn't the case. If the families have something in their apartments that is broken, and they need help getting the property managers to fix it, they know I can assist them."

"The difference between what I'm doing now working at a non-profit, and what I used to do, is that what I'm working on now is so much more rewarding. I'm making a difference with the community, versus making more money for shareholders. This job also provides me with more flexibility as well, which is important to me as a working mother."

I asked Elizabeth if one or two families stood out with her that she helped make a difference. "One family I'm working with now has a father who is a cancer patient. He is a veteran, but he currently cannot work because of his cancer treatment. The mother has had to stop working because of complications with her third pregnancy. The family went to live with her family, but they were too crowded. Crisis Assistance Ministry took them in right before the birth of their third child and helped give them housing. Once the father is done with chemotherapy, and the baby is old enough, they should both be back working and earning money again. In the meantime, they needed our help to get them through a really tough time. They are really an amazing family and have really broadened my horizons."

"Also, I'm thrilled to know a mom of a 12-year-old who is working with our program. They had the choice of picking two apartments to live in. One was an apartment in a wonderful neighborhood with a terrific school system; the other was a gorgeous apartment that has just been rehabbed, but it is in a really challenging neighborhood. They picked the apartment that had just been rehabbed, because the quality of the apartment is great. The woman is a small business owner of a cleaning company, and she loves the idea of making a difference in the community and helping it begin its turnaround. I was surprised at her choice, but I found it inspiring."

When you do something like Elizabeth did, such as volunteering to help the homeless, you'll see the blessings in your own life. Even though times may be uncertain, and you may not be sure what's going to happen to you, hopefully you're coming home to your own home, with furniture, belongings, and food in the refrigerator. Working in the community helps you to be thankful for what you do have.

Working in the community helps you to be thankful for what you do have.

When you're networking with the people who run your organization, as well as working alongside others, let them know you're looking for a job. The more people who know this, the better your chances are for success.

Unemployed and Under-Employed

Millions of people right now are on the unemployment lines. It's a worrying time in our economy, and it's likely to take a while for employment numbers to return to healthier levels.

It's very easy to be depressed and discouraged. Hopefully this will only be a blip in your life. Instead of seeing it as a disaster, allow yourself to see this as an opportunity to find your passion, your calling, and new ways to be creative. With free time away from the daily grind, it's possible to just stop, look around, and see what is going on in the world. Utilize your time as constructively as you can. Think about what are the two or three things you want to focus your energies on.

See this as an opportunity to find your passion, your calling, and new ways to be creative.

You need time every day to be organized about looking for a new job, looking at career websites, Facebook, Linked In, networking with professional groups, and following leads. Then, it's time for giving back.

Here's one example of using the time that you wouldn't normally have if you were working, and making it work for something that so many can benefit from.

Let's say back when you were working, you had your house burglarized. You were gone so much on business that your house was easy prey. Although you repaired the doors and your insurance replaced your items, you remember how awful it felt when you came home and saw that flat screen missing from your wall. You hated the idea of burglars in your house.

You decide to investigate starting up a Neighborhood Watch Program to cut down on crime in your area. With your new free time, you can contact your local police department and ask how to get started. You can set up a meeting with the homeowners association, go to different neighbors, and see whether there is an interest among a large enough group of people to make it viable. After your meetings with the police department, you are able to give a solid presentation about the benefits of the Neighborhood Watch.

After a couple of months of your hard work, the program is up and running. The signs are posted in your neighborhood. You can see how your efforts have benefited your entire neighborhood by making it safer. None of this would have happened if you hadn't had the free time to make it work.

One thing that becomes clear is that life never takes a straight path. You might think that you have your life all figured out, and then a curve ball gets thrown at you.

I met Dexter Durrante through the Wounded Warrior Project. This is a program for Disabled Veterans that gives financial and other types of assistance for them and their families. Dexter is a divorced father of five who never intended to be out of work, but then a terrible accident left him blinded.

"I was in the Army for 20 years. During a routine training event on the demolition range, we were cleaning up, and I saw a shockwave coming off the fire. That was the last thing I saw."

"When it happened, I felt like I didn't want to live. I felt like I couldn't function without my eyes, and I wished I were dead. It was a really depressing time. I wanted to just lie around and feel sorry for myself. A turning point came less than a month later, in rehab, when I learned a bunch of things that I could do without my sight. It's been almost three years since my accident, and I'm so much happier to be alive."

"I ran into a man who was blinded who became a great inspiration to me. He still runs marathons, gets around, works on the computer, is married, and has kids. He was a big help to me. We would have group sessions and just sit and talk."

Dexter with guide dog, Shepherd, and friends John and Rashe, from the
Wounded Warrior Project, with me at a baseball game

"I became independent thanks to my guide dog; this was life-changing. I may not be able to drive, but I have a lifelong companion. Every time I turn, go up, or go down he is there for me. The only thing he requires is for me to feed him, brush him, and give him water. Getting him was a big turning point in my life."

"Having a good support system is also invaluable. My wife and I split up after the accident, and initially I had 400 people coming to visit me wanting to do something. However, as time went by, those numbers dwindled to a couple of buddies who I knew I could count on. They call regularly and check up on me."

"I retired a couple of years after the accident as a Master Sergeant. I want to be a blind rehab instructor for veterans. As a blind man, I think I could provide insight, and it would give me a chance to give back to my fellow veterans. I'm going to get my Masters to get a job with the VA, I'm exercising, and I'm training for triathlons. I try to do the best I can."

You never know what kind of challenge life is going to throw at you, whether it be unemployment or an accident like Dexter's, that forces you to rethink and relearn everything that you do. Stories like these show that resilience and paying it forward reap rewards.

Retired People

When you're retired, you've got to keep yourself busy and your mind young for longevity as well as overall mental and physical health. You've had a lifetime of experiences that has given you time to know what's close to your heart. It's really important that if you are able to do so, make a commitment to volunteer.

Seniors relish spending their free time doing a variety of fun activities, as well as spending time with family and friends. Try to work volunteering in with these activities.

For instance, instead of a bus-load of seniors going off to try their hands at slots and blackjack once a month, why not take a bus load to work at a soup kitchen? If you were a music teacher for your career, think about playing at a place like a nursing home to bring some joy and music to the elderly. A former banker, who never had the time to be involved with different activities, had always been interested in helping the Special Olympics. Now she has the time to be involved with that incredible organization.

When you're older and you start to notice that you're losing people close to you, there's a sadness that people who have meant so much to you are passing on. You could go through times of sadness and emptiness, like you are untethered without your lifelong work to keep you busy. It might be easy to fall into a dark place.

Volunteering helps keep you young. As you're working, you get to hear daily goings-on and family stories from those around you. You might be able to share your experiences with those folks younger than you - talk to them about growing up during the Depression. Talk about how much things cost when you were a teenager: gas was 5 cents a gallon, and movies cost a dime. Teach them about life before cell phones, remote controls, and the internet! You will become very valuable as a friend to younger people; you can share your wisdom and connect to the current generation. Your young friends might, in turn, be able to convince you about the wonders of a DVR and show you how to skip commercials. They may also be able to help program your cell phone, and they can show you all the fun tools on it that you never have heard of.

Bill Gerhart is a terrific example of a retired man who found a whole new life in volunteering.

"I spent 35 years in the electrical industry, and I retired in 2007. I recognized that during my working life I had not done a lot of volunteer work. I was determined that as long as I was active, I was going to do volunteer work in Charlotte. In our newspaper there is an annual pull-out section that lists all the non- profits, who they are, and what they do. My wife and I had worked for the Red Cross over the years. I knew that I was probably going to work with them, but I was looking for one more group."

"I found MedAssist. It's a working pharmacy that dispenses drugs to those who have very low income and no insurance. I started working with them until my wife became ill with leukemia. I saw first-hand what the Red Cross had done for her. We went through seven months at Duke Medical Center while she had chemotherapy and a stem cell transplant. There were platelet blood transfusions, and we always noticed the Red Cross people at the outpatient clinic on a daily basis."

"When my wife passed away in 2009, I stayed busy. With MedAssist, I work one-half day a week regularly, and then I do other things as they come up, such as picking up medicine at a doctor's office. I also speak at United Way campaigns on behalf of MedAssist."

"For the Red Cross, I had always worked in the donor room, doing one or two sessions a week. Now I also have transportation work as well for people who need to go to doctors' appointments, and I do that for a half day. I also volunteer 3-5 sessions a week for the bloodmobile. "

"I went into volunteering on the theory that I hadn't paid my dues in doing things like this – I traveled a lot and we moved around when I was working. We had always donated money, but that's just a small piece of what non-profits need. They need people to do the work. Without volunteers, things don't get done. I was not interested in getting in an organization and sitting on a board. I wanted to be on the ground and do the work that needed to be done."

We had always donated money, but that's just a small piece of what non-profits need. They need people to do the work.

"Now I feel like I have four or five different families with the Red Cross and MedAssist. The contact with people is invaluable. You can't sit home and twiddle your thumbs; you need to be out and in contact with people."

5 things you can do today
5 things you can do today
5 things you can do today
5 things you can do today
5 things you can do today
5 things you can do today
5 things you can do today
5 things you can do today
5 things you can do today

5 things you can do today

Spotlight: Helping Military Personnel and Veterans.

There are many active military personnel, veterans, and families who need assistance for many reasons. There are husbands, wives, and fathers serving overseas, wounded veterans, and veterans who are on limited budgets. There are so many ways to help these people, but here are five ideas to start with:

1 Buy gift cards from pharmacies for veterans to help pay for prescriptions.

2 Give tickets to sporting events through programs like Wounded Warrior Project.

3 Assemble care packages and cards for troops serving overseas.

4 Arrange babysitters for wives and husbands whose spouses are serving oversease, so that they can have a night out.

5 Donate computer cameras for families to enable live video conferences overseas.

chapterseven
chapterseven
chapterseven
chapterseven
chapterseven
chapterseven
chapterseven
chapterseven
chapterseven
chapterseven
chapterseven

Making a Career
out of Helping

A car crashes late at night on a busy city street, and the young man trapped inside prays for help to come quickly. A child shows up nervous on the first day of third grade, not knowing what to expect from her new teacher. A family hit by lay-offs ends up losing their house and struggles to find a place to live. A neighborhood is gripped by fear over crime. A mother has a 7-year-old with developmental problems, but she doesn't know how to get the services she needs to help him. A child becomes ill with a chronic disease, and her family is desperate to find a cure.

There are amazing people out in our community every day working full-time to help people and to make our world a better place. They are in public safety: firefighters, police officers, and EMTs; they are working at non-profits helping charities; they are teachers, helping our children to learn and become good citizens; they are clergy, helping people find a relationship with God and the community. Often, these caretakers are making less money than they could in the corporate world, but the satisfaction and gratification that come from seeing positive change in the community far outweigh the desire to become financially better off.

What draws people to do the work that they do, and what inspires them to carry on when the problems they try to solve seem insurmountable? I am continually fascinated by these questions. You may find that after participating in your volunteer work your perspective begins to change about what you are doing with your career. These stories might make it possible for you to envision the possibilities for making a career out of helping. This can reap so many rewards for all involved. I think their stories are remarkably inspiring in very different ways.

> **You may find that after participating in your volunteer work your perspective begins to change about what you are doing with your career work.**

A Police Officer Pays it Forward

Demarco Jeter is a police officer I have known for eleven years. He is one of my personal heroes. His story shows how a difficult childhood can be turned around through sports and the attention of a few caring individuals. "I grew up in a house with a park that was only three quarters of a mile away. When I was a kid, it was just somewhere to go to play with my friends. That was where I began to learn how to play football and basketball. I had never played football before. I liked the toughness it took to do well; in my neighborhood, you had to be tough. Some of the coaches were police officers, but that didn't really register with me at first. I was just trying to play football, basketball, and baseball."

"When I got to high school, I was able to look back on what playing on these teams did for me. I grew up in a home with an alcoholic for an adult male figure. Playing at that park allowed me to get away from all the problems and abuse at home. I could mentally and physically be away from home and out of a neighborhood where there were a lot of fights, stabbings, and other crimes. Everything I saw at football was positive. This was due to the Police Activities League (then known as the Police Athletic League)."

"They made a difference in my life. A lot of my friends who didn't play sports wound up in trouble. They weren't on the high school teams, and they weren't achieving good grades at school. They ended up being some of the drug dealers in the neighborhood, dropouts, or going to jail."

"I played football in college – I thought I was going to turn pro and give back monetarily to the struggling kids and Police Activities League in my neighborhood. Our youth teams were the ones that had run down uniforms or off-brand sneakers. We used that as our motivation. My mindset in college was that once I turned pro, I was going to go back and make sure that they had decent uniforms. But as it turned out, I wasn't pro material, and now money is not my big contribution to the Police Activities League."

"I have always wanted to be out making a difference in the world. So I became a police officer." I asked DeMarco how he keeps motivated. "With 911 calls, you deal with people's problems all day long, from flat tires to homicides. Nobody's sitting down and offering you a slice of pie and a cup of coffee – it's always an emergency. I have always disliked the idea of looking out a window or being stuck behind a computer screen. I'm out there speaking to people on the streets, traveling around the community, and finding out what's going on. I get gratification from knowing that I've made someone's problems a little bit easier. People look you in the eye and say, 'Thank you.' As with a lot of officers, it's the small battles that give us gratification."

"I don't think I could ever match the legacy of the man who coached me when I was a kid – he spent 33 years coach-

Demarco Jeter delivering his half team speech for the
Pop Warner Championship game

---

ing. But I want the kids to remember that I played there, and I came back to help. I want them to do the same. When I first started out, I wasn't fortunate enough to have a regular schedule. I would periodically show up at practices where I grew up, and the coach said it was o.k. if I showed up when I could. When I went to a federal task force, my supervisor was more than willing to let me attend the practices. I started coaching football with one of the coaches who had helped raise me out there on the fields. When he passed away, I became the head coach for the football team – that was very profound for me."

Demarco also referees for basketball games and is the assistant coach for the baseball team. "I support those kids, and even if they don't go off to college and become a CEO,

I want them to come down, participate, and say hello. I want them to think that it isn't to give back, it's to give forward. A lot of these kids aren't fortunate enough to live down the road from the park like I was. Sometimes they ride the bus, which I don't think is safe or financially good for them. If I'm available, I'll pick them up myself. Our chief allows us to use our squad cars for that purpose, if it needs to be done. For these kids, there's a lot more to playing on a team than just throwing and catching a ball – it's about discipline, teamwork, punctuality, and responsibility. I try to show them that this is true for me too - they can depend on me. If they need cleats, I have four pairs in the trunk of my car. If their parent(s) can afford them, they can buy them from me, and if not, I just give them away. I ordered all types of exercise equipment for the kids to use for training. Sometimes I get money from friends or coworkers who might want to contribute. It's all going to come back to us, one way or the other."

> **"For these kids, there's a lot more to playing on a team than just throwing and catching a ball – it's about discipline, teamwork, punctuality, and responsibility."**

I love Demarco's story not only because he is a hero working as a police officer helping people in crisis situations. I also love it because when he is off-duty, he is also helping out the community with the Police Activities League. He is a firm believer in paying it forward because he was helped out as a young boy. Demarco gives his time to coach, helps with rides to practice, spends his spare cash to buy equipment for the kids, and sets a great example of being a man who is dependable and caring. He also demonstrates to a part of the community who may not always respect the law that police officers are trustworthy and are there to look after the best interests of the neighborhood.

Evolving Personal Goals with a Desire to Help

Going to a small village in Africa to help the residents grow better crops and improve survival rates for their children may seem way out of the realm of possibility for most of us, who may be unwilling to leave family and friends.

Laura Casoni, however, knew from an early age what she wanted to do. "It goes back to when we went to visit my mom's family in Italy where she grew up. They lived in a small farming village where the economy was supported by a local nunnery. They relied on each other and the land. They would be considered poor. I was thinking about what the difference was between this lifestyle in Italy and that of my mother who moved away: it was opportunity. Opportunity gave my mother a chance to gain wealth and have a totally different life. When I watched TV and saw severe poverty on the news, I wondered what that opportunity could give to people. I decided I wanted to join the Peace Corps. It would be an adventure, as well as an opportunity to change the lives of the people who most needed it."

"The impact I had on the small village in Africa where I was stationed was the introduction of new ideas and products to incorporate into their lives and ultimately experience change. That change is really possible: slow, but possible, if we're willing to embrace new things. The impact on me was unbelievable. The best things that came out of it were the friendships and the knowledge that no matter what your economic status or where you live, we all grapple with the same issues and have the same dreams and desires. When we start to see each other that way, it changes the way we see the world."

"We all grapple with the same issues and have the same dreams and desires. When we start to see each other that way, it changes the way we see the world."

Laura came back after two years of service. "I needed to start making money, and I also decided that I needed to feel challenged in a different way. I went to graduate school and then into medical research. My experience in corporate America is that the money is nice, and you can get easily caught up in that. However, the politics are draining, and at the end of the day, the maneuvering is not about what's best for the company, or about what's best for the community, but it's what is the best for me."

"I found that I had that desire again to do something that was bigger than myself. I could challenge myself again by going to work for Goodwill. I'm now working to initiate their micro-lending domestic fund. The program seeks economic development through small business activities. The objective is to provide alternate financing, in a way that is helpful to small business owners. By creating opportunities for them, it gives everybody opportunities."

"Goodwill is very open to innovation, more so than anywhere I've worked in corporate America. Because every one who works at Goodwill has a common mission, to benefit our society, we thoroughly think through and research the impact of our actions."

With her sharp mind and compassionate nature, Laura has made a difference both at home and abroad.

Clergy Taking Risks and Finding Balance

One of the issues that people get hung up on when they think about working in the community is the possibility of failure. What if I do something wrong? What if I do more harm than good? What if the people I want to help don't want anything to do with me?

Chris Payne, Senior Pastor at New Charlotte Church, knows where this feeling comes from. He is a married father of three who left a comfortable existence as a pastor at a large, well-established church to found a new church on a different side of town. "We fear failing and letting people down, so we use it as a reason to not get involved. One of the things I've learned, as I transition from being a pastor at a large church to founding our own small church, is to give it everything you can. It will be used for good in other peoples lives, as well as in your own lives. If you're following your calling and are passionate about it, you're not going to fail. Even if the outcome is different than what you pictured, it will make a difference. The input is where we can release a lot of our fears of failure."

> **"If you're following your calling and are passionate about it, you're not going to fail. Even if the outcome is different than what you pictured, it will make a difference."**

I was curious about how people get involved, so I asked Chris how he became a pastor. "I got into the ministry from a sense of call to help other people and to give of myself. I had a desire to help other people. I feel like part of what we do is to connect people to God and send them out into the world to love their neighbor."

Not everybody knows what kind of work makes up a member of the clergy's day apart from Sundays, and apparently, they sometimes don't quite know themselves. "Our days can be so different every single week, and we have to order our lives around the unpredictable and the unexpected. We have to step out of our own schedule and desires of how we would like our day to go. With preaching, praying, services, performing ceremonies, or visiting someone who's ill, a lot of service has to do with the ministry of availability. We have the regular part of our days: study, prayer, sermons to write, services, meeting with our staff, and the running of the business side of the church. Then we have relationships with the people in our congregation. There are deaths, births, trouble in relationships, as well as good things that happen in people's lives. As a pastor, it's an honor to be asked to be a part of both the good and the bad."

Because of the nature of the unexpected calls that can come for a clergy member, I wondered how it was possible to maintain balance as a husband and father. "I have had several guides who have mentored balance for me. The needs of this world can be all-consuming, and I do think that setting boundaries is very important when you are helping other people. We've tried to build a culture in our community to acknowledge that families are first and foremost. The Bible says that if someone isn't able to provide for their family, they certainly cannot provide for the world. If I'm out doing 100 community projects, I'm not paying proper attention to my family. I have to acknowledge that there's only so much I can do, and while I try and withhold nothing, this is where I end, and you have to begin. Sometimes I have to say no."

"I think serving with a small group is very important because you can learn from each other and help people keep in balance. You can talk to the other person and say, 'Hey, you've lost perspective.'"

Chris's message about being available to help, balancing community work with family, and taking risks are all ideas we can use.

A Whole New World for Diabetics

There is nothing more frightening for a parent to have a child who is sick and in the hospital. For the 30,000 people a year who are diagnosed with juvenile (also known as Type 1) diabetes, their whole way of living each day is forever changed because of this disease; a cure has not yet been discovered. A significant number of those diagnosed are children.

A phone call will go out to the Juvenile Diabetes Research Foundation with every diagnosis from the hospital.

Sally Langan is a Development Manager for the Juvenile Diabetes Research Foundation in charge of outreach. "About 15 times a month, somebody is diagnosed with juvenile diabetes in our area. Our mentor program then kicks in. We have a family, with a child of a similar age, volunteer to visit that newly diagnosed child at the hospital." For those families in the hospital, this is a lifeline. "These families are overwhelmed by this life-changing diagnosis. They can't believe that they are in this situation, and everyday life seems like a different world. Our volunteers help show these new families that they will get through this, and they will have a new normal. The responses that we get from those families who go through the mentor program are terrific. It's wonderful when those families want to give back as well and become mentors for other families."

Juvenile diabetes is a disease that needs to be intensively managed 24 hours a day with correct dosing of insulin shots and counting carbohydrates. There is an ever-present risk for severe complications if mistakes are made, as well as a lifelong host of risk factors for other problems if diabetes is not managed closely. Parents and children can feel that it will be impossible to ever feel like they can have fun again.

That is also where the JDRF steps in. Families are connected through the organization for networking events, research, and fundraising for a cure. A community is created. Sally found out about what the JDRF can do when she got an internship there in college. "I could see the amount of good the foundation was doing, both in raising money for a cure and funding research, as well as connecting families living with Type 1 diabetes. As an organization, it's part of our responsibility to be the vehicle through which events get planned, house information for the use of those who need it, and offer up support networks to families to connect with others. When I graduated, serendipitously, a position became available in San Antonio. When I left there and moved to Charlotte, a position also became available at the JDRF there. It's made me think, for many reasons, that this is the right path for me."

"What is so great about this job is seeing the good that you're doing. On our big fundraising days, it's always so amazing to see families coming to the event together for the same purpose of finding a cure." For Sally, working in non-profits was always something she knew she was going to do. "I grew up in the world of non-profits. My mother was a director of different non-profits in Nashville. I always admired what she was able to do in the community through her work on boards and volunteering."

Now Sally is following in her mother's footsteps of helping the community. Her work at the JDRF encourages and supports families, while working to raise money to find a cure for this terrible disease.

Giving Up the Corporate World

Whereas Sally Langan always knew the kind of role she wanted after graduation, Tim Brown came to the realization that he was in the wrong job, in, of all places, France. His experience there made him see what his corporate job was not doing for him. "I started off as an IT consultant with Price Waterhouse Coopers. I was consulting for eight or nine years, and I enjoyed the corporate life. One assignment sent me to France for six months. Living there and seeing their way of life opened my eyes. In France they work to live, whereas in the U.S., we live to work. When I got back to the States, I realized I didn't want to work to make money for me and my company. It wasn't fulfilling. I just didn't want to do that for the next 20 years."

"I wanted to do something that made me happy, and I wanted to do things for other people. I had always wanted to be a part of the fire department, and while living in Chicago,

I applied for a position in Charlotte. Everything just clicked, and I got in. In 2003 I became a firefighter, and in 2009 I became a captain. I love being a firefighter and knowing that when somebody is in trouble, you can help them."

For Tim, the unknown of what the next call will bring keeps him fresh through his 24-hour shifts. "Every call is different, and you never know how urgent it's going to be. It could be relatively low in urgency, such as someone with a bruised knee, or a new mom with a crying baby who isn't sure what she's experiencing is normal. On the other hand, it could be a full-on emergency –assault, rape, or fire. There is never a call that we go on that is the same as the last, and that spurs most firefighters on. For instance, you may have somebody experiencing an allergic reaction, and the next thing you know, they're going downhill fast. It puts you into a ramped-up state and keeps your adrenaline going. You're always there to help, and you're always on your toes to get the job done."

"There is never a call that we go on that is the same as the last, and that spurs most firefighters on."

When he's not on duty, Tim also finds a way to align what he finds fulfilling, working out, with helping people. "I'm also a personal trainer, and I think it goes hand-in-hand with firefighting because it's about helping people. I had one client who was 310 pounds, and within the last year, I helped him to lose over 50 pounds. It was life-changing for him. Everything in life changes when you lose weight to become healthier. You can take long walks without losing your breath or play on the floor with your kids. It also opens up so many possibilities in your life by boosting your confidence."

"Firefighting and personal training help me to feel good about myself, as opposed to making money to make myself feel good. I don't want to be on my deathbed, look back, and see that everything I've done is just for myself. I want people to be able to look back and say that I have made a difference." The desire to make a difference is a powerful motivator for many who work full-time in the community.

Comfort Makes Confidence in the Classroom

Can you remember a special teacher who made a difference in your life? I had many teachers inspire me in so many different ways. So did Courtney Evans, who is now a public school teacher. "I always really enjoyed school, and I still remember every single teacher I had starting in kindergarten. Having had such positive experiences at school helped pushed me towards a career in education. Ever since I was little, I always wanted to be a teacher. It was really the only career I considered, although I briefly looked at other more lucrative careers just to make sure I wasn't missing out on something. But my junior year of high school, I interned at an elementary school, and I was hooked. I applied to Appalachian State, which has an excellent program for teaching. From student teaching positions to interning, I always had positive experiences, which led me to know that I was on the right path. Truthfully, I never really pictured my life any other way than working with children."

When you walk into Mrs. Evans' third grade class, it's a model for the perfectly-run schoolroom. The children are quietly and respectfully doing their work. Every child looks happy and excited to be there. I asked her how she is able to accomplish this. "At the beginning of the year, I tell the children real things about me, my life, and my experiences, so that they can get to know me. Then I ask questions about their lives, their families, and their interests. I emphasize to the children how important they are to me by learning their first and last names by the end of the first day. They quiz me on it, and I get it right every year. If you let children know the rules of the classroom, what's expected of them, and the classroom routines, they can feel comfortable knowing they are doing the right thing. They don't worry about putting a foot out of place. We even discuss the rules for the seemingly smallest of things. It could be a question of when they can sharpen their pencils, or we might develop a hand signal if they need to use the restroom if I'm in the middle of teaching. We talk about the fact that our classroom is a family because we spend a lot of time together. While I don't expect everyone to be best friends, we all need to respect each other."

As a career, teaching is satisfying in many ways. One example of this is when you see a child leave the classroom at the end of the year after achieving so much. "One little girl had just been diagnosed with ADD at the end of second grade, which is late to make that diagnosis. As a result, she'd had a pretty rough school career. She and I were able to make a connection, and she was comfortable enough with me to ask questions and not shy away from hard work. She had tremendous growth in the third grade, thanks to the treatment for her ADD and the good relationship we had. The longer I teach, the more I realize I've got to keep my teaching style the same – personal, yet fun, and at the same time the children know when it's time to get down to business. That's been the key to growth in my classroom that maybe that they hadn't had before."

Courtney also recognizes that her job is an important one outside the classroom as well. "I feel that the role of a teacher is an important one in the community; it's not a regular job where you clock out at the end of the day. I'm never really off duty – I might see one of my kids in the grocery store or out with their families at a restaurant. I see some of the children more than their parents do, so we're not just educating. We're teaching manners, life skills, and lessons that go beyond textbooks. I also try to make sure the children know that I'm an active member of the community outside of school. If I'm participating in Race for the Cure, or if I'm doing an outreach program at my church, we talk about it. I want them to see that I get involved, and I hope that will rub off on them. Some people look at teaching as a job, but I see it as almost like a lifestyle. You're a leader, a role model, and somebody who cares about their community."

> **"I see some of the children more than their parents do, so we're not just educating. We're teaching manners, life skills, and lessons that go beyond textbooks."**

We need more role models in our community to help show children what good people do in and out of their jobs.

An Advocate for Families

Christine Luppino works for a non-profit group that works with her county to help developmentally-challenged children and adults, as well as supporting their families. She knows that these families need a lot of direction on how to advocate for themselves. Christine is a big believer in social justice, and she feels that it is her life's purpose to help people have equality not only within the law, but also in society.

"These families are often grieving and in turmoil. I feel strongly that people's problems don't exist in isolation; parents aren't going to be able to worry about their child's lack of age-appropriate vocabulary if they don't have a place to live or food on the table. We need to be able to make all our systems work together to solve this family's needs."

> **"People's problems don't exist in isolation."**

I asked Christine how she decided to pursue a career in social work. "I have always been interested in working with children, and I was looking to go back to school and find programs in the area where I could help kids. I had an acquaintance who knew about a psychology program, which focused on kids but in a family systems way. It was a very practical, results-oriented program. I came out of graduate school being qualified to do something specific, and what I love about my job is that there are always more things to learn. It's challenging to examine all the different ways to solve problems."

Social work is not for those who are looking to have lots of material extras in life, and it can be hard to make ends meet. "When things get hard, nothing is going right, and you don't get paid anything, I think about selling out. It would be just for one year, though – it could never be long term. Sometimes I think about getting in the car, driving west, and starting a Christmas tree farm. But life would be boring if I didn't get to work with all these families; I get to see so many different slices of life. Sometimes people I spend time with haven't had access to a wide range of ideas, and they don't know why it's important to extend unemployment benefits or have affordable child care,. They don't understand how all of these things are connected to a family's ability to succeed. This job gives you incredible perspective on things."

Christine and I talked about whether there were any families who inspired her on days when she might be feeling a bit down. "I'm definitely not supposed to have favorites. You develop really strong relationships with families, but what has been really motivating for me is working with immigrant families. This is a group of people who really needs extra help. You can see so much progress; they really absorb what you're telling them, and you see that it's making a difference."

"I had data entry jobs early in my career, and I wondered how I got so removed from actually doing something where I can see results. I was just typing numbers! What I do now has an impact right then and there. There are consequences to what I do that help keep me fresh for every call. If I do my job right, people get help, and if I do my job incorrectly, people get hurt. I am passionate about what I do, and I enjoy connecting to the world and advocating for people."

It was such an honor to spend time talking with these amazing people who spend every day making a difference and having a tremendous impact in our community. They are very special people who deserve our thanks. The next time you see a police officer, a social worker, a teacher, or somebody who has made helping into their life's work, say how much you appreciate what they do.

5 things you can do today
5 things you can do today
5 things you can do today
5 things you can do today
5 things you can do today
5 things you can do today
5 things you can do today
5 things you can do today
5 things you can do today
5 things you can do today

5 things you can do today

Spotlight: Thank Someone Who Works in Your Community.

Many who work in the community spend long hours on the job, sometimes risking their lives, and receive limited financial compensation. Make their day a little nicer by showing how much you appreciate them:

1 Take food to your local fire station and police department.

2 Give a gift card to a teacher.

3 Give a monetary donation to a children's missionary trip.

4 Leave a thank-you note for your postal worker with a gift inside.

5 If you're home on a summer day when your garbage and recycling gets picked up, have some icy cold water bottles for the workers.

chapter eight
chapter eight
chapter eight
chapter eight
chapter eight
chapter eight
chapter eight
chapter eight
chapter eight
chapter eight
chapter eight

Organizing Events

This is a special chapter specifically focused on planning and organizing fundraising events. If you have never thrown an event, get ready to have fun, be challenged, and recruit lots of friends to help out. If you have put on a fundraiser before, I have gathered lots of fresh ideas that I hope will give you new revenue-generating possibilities to raise even more money the next time.

We're going to use a theoretical event to help illustrate how you would go about planning one from start to finish. Keep in mind that the list of things you'll need to organize is long, and there will be more items to think about that will come up. Just remember, you'll never have a more satisfying day.

An Illustrative Cause

I wanted to make our sample cause something that everyone could relate to. Throughout the country for the past couple of decades, and even more so because of the current recession, funding for sports programs and arts education in schools has been slashed. In my city of Charlotte, the school system now requires that students pay a fee in order to participate in after-school sports starting in middle school. Physical education, which students used to attend a few times a week, is now down to only once a week. Surely a direct result of this is the rising numbers of overweight and obese children around the country.

Arts funding is in a nose-dive as electives such as orchestra, band, drama, photography, fine arts, choir, and more are eliminated and determined as not essential to the core curriculum. As a result, students themselves have to pay more in order to get educated in these areas, or they go outside the school system to find these programs.

If the school systems require that students pay for sports and arts programs, a lot of families aren't in the position to be able to purchase equipment or supplies. What would be the best way to provide scholarships to those kids who need them, as well as keeping the tradition alive of school sports, bands, and theatre productions?

What Should the Event Be?

Casual or formal, party or lecture, walk or dinner, there are so many fun ways to raise money where people can enjoy themselves, while knowing that their money is going to a good cause. Here are some ideas of events that you could throw for your cause:

FORMAL
- Black tie dinner
- Cocktail reception
- Famous lecture/speaker
- Luncheon
- Casino night

INFORMAL/KIDS
- Barbeque/cookout

- Oyster roast/clam bake
- Bouncy-castles and clowns/Carnival
- Day at the Zoo/Museum
- Potluck
- Disco Night
- Bingo

SPORTS
- Golf tournament
- Beach volleyball
- Fishing tournament
- Bike-a-thon
- 5k walk

When thinking of an event, you have to think of who your supporters are most likely to be, and think about what they would enjoy doing. Is this an event for grown-ups or families? This will affect admission prices, as well as determine the timing and place for the event.

For our theoretical fundraiser, let's think of our audience and cause, and then decide what would be an appropriate and fun way to raise money. Since the schools and schoolchildren are going to benefit, a festival at the school would be a logical way to go. Thinking about logistics, this would be a place that is easy to get to and easy to find, with streets that can likely accommodate a lot of traffic and parking. Convenience is key for all those who might want to attend.

Think about your school property – where is the best location to hold a festival? Depending on the size of your school, you will generally have some sort of football field/ stadium or track area, which would make a great open space. There are also the cafeteria facilities at the school, which you might be able to utilize in order to produce food for the event.

Getting Started

The first step in planning an event is getting organized. Write down everything that you need to plan, and keep it with contact numbers and ideas in one place. I have a gigantic tote bag with my important events folder that I lug with me everywhere.

Talk to everyone you know (see Chapter Three) and start gathering friends, colleagues, neighbors, and families to help you out. You will need a lot of support, so start polling people on which roles they would like to fill for your event.

Set a goal for the amount of money you want to raise. Calculate how many children are in sports, what percentage of those might need assistance, and how much per child that will cost. This number may change, but at least you've got a ballpark goal.

When you have figured out the location you would like to use, you need to approach the head of the facility and find out what is involved to use that place. Are there any fees, and if so, can they be waived? If that place is unwilling to work with you, move on until you find the right place. Once you do, the person in charge will be able to give you all the contact people you need to touch base with as you move forward.

In the case of our school festival, you would need to share the idea with the school's principal, see whether he or she is comfortable with you using the school for this event, check dates, and see what other kind of approval you might need.

Explain your goals, sketch the outline of what you would like to see happen in order to raise the money, and talk about the facilities you envision being able to use. Find out from the principal who would need to sign off on this plan – perhaps the PTA, the school board or superintendent, and the Athletic Director whose fields or facilities you might want to use. Be flexible. Although it's a fundraiser for the students of his/her school, it's difficult for us to envision the types of bureaucratic hoops that you might have to go through in order to accomplish this type of event. You are going to need every "i" dotted and every "t" crossed.

Hopefully you've now gotten the principal excited about your idea, and you also have convinced her of your abilities to work with others to make the event a success. You've gotten feedback on some of your ideas, and a line of communication has been opened to discuss further issues as they come up.

When you call your meeting with the next group of people – the school board, the PTA, the coaches, the band leader, the boosters, or the choir director, you can talk to them about what you would like to do and why. Gain their support, and you can add more names to your committee. If people at that meeting are too busy, get recommendations and mailing lists. If there are booster clubs, see if you can get these people involved. See if the principal or the PTA can send out an email using their lists of parents.

Naming Your Cause

You will need a clever, catchy name for your cause that aligns with what you are trying to accomplish. Give your cause a name early on so you and others can start referring to it, and this will give you time to think of logos and catchy designs. Ask a friend who is either good at graphic design or has a great, user-friendly computer application to help you get started on your design.

Timing the Event

Timing an event is extremely important. You need to think of the time of year, day of the week, and time of day. You want to make sure that you pick a date for the event that gives you enough time to get everything done. The date will also have to make sense as far as what you are raising money for, as well as what kind of event it is. You wouldn't have a cookout in Maine in January, but there would be nothing better than a lobster roast in July.

If you are new to putting on a fundraiser, ask yourself whether you are giving yourself enough time to put all the elements together. As an experienced fundraiser, I find three months is a good amount of time; everyone is pressed to get stuff done, and nobody gets complacent. Six months, however, might make me think that I have all the time in the world to assemble the pieces of the puzzle,. I might end up getting far behind and off-schedule.

For the date, think about whether enough people will be in town to attend your event. Make sure it's not on a holiday weekend when folks are out of town, during graduation season, or when people are busy preparing for the holidays. Many people are away sporadically during the summer season, but if you give people enough advance notice, they'll try and not make plans for when your event is going to be.

Also, the time of day is vitally important. If children are involved, clearly it cannot be a late-night event. If it is an adults-only crowd, there is a sweet-spot of time after work ends, and people can either go home or go out. If you allow people enough time to go home and change out of their work clothes before your event starts, you might find that people don't show up because they have gotten too comfortable at home to go back out again.

For our theoretical event, if you are trying to sponsor children for the next school year, your event needs to be before school kicks off. So let's say we pick July, after the 4th, when people are done going on vacation, but pre-season practices for fall sports haven't started yet.

When picking out the day, you need to figure out which day of the week will get the most attendance. Since our sample event is at a school, our only choices would be on a Friday night, Saturday, or Sunday. We'll stick with Saturday because Sundays are usually reserved for church and family time.

The time of day for our festival would be from 10-2. Because this is an event for families, this would give people a range of hours to stop by and hopefully have some food.

Save the Date

Once you decide the type of event, the name, the date, and the time it will occur, you can start sending out "Save the Date" notices. Get the word out to as many people as you can possibly think of, and make sure that others are doing the same.

Raising Money

There are many different ways to raise money at your event. Take some time to consider all of the revenue streams that could be a part of the day:

- Raffle tickets – have a donated item be the prize (a flat-screen TV, a trip, a vacation house).
- Ticketed entry - Is this an event to which people will need a ticket to get in? If so, everything the ticket buyer receives should be specified – whether it be dinner, open bar, hot hors d'oeuvres. Make sure your attendees know what is and is not included in the price of their ticket.
- Food and Drink - If your event is a pay-as-you-go affair, you will need to figure out the food and drink you are serving, as well as how much to charge the guests for these items.
- Donations - You need to have areas where people can write checks or give cash donations.
- Live and Silent Auction items - These items need to be gathered from businesses and services around town, displayed at your event, and then auctioned off.
- Rides/activities

Bringing in professional sports memorabilia can raise lots of money at a Live Auction.

Volunteers cooking donated hamburgers and hotdogs.

We'll discuss each of these ideas in depth on the following pages. You do not want an opportunity to miss out on getting more money once people are at your event to make it a success.

You will need a revenue committee. One of those people should be good at accounting and trustworthy. Decide whether or not, throughout the day of your event, you are going to be depositing cash in the bank to keep it safe. If that is not an option, how will you be safeguarding the money? Next, divide up the tasks of getting donations for each of these sources of revenues. You will need outgoing people to solicit goods and services for raffle and auction items, or you need to find people who are willing to try on behalf of a great cause.

You will also need a food committee. Think about the food you would like to serve (in the event of a ticketed entry) or sell (in the pay-as-you-go model), and try to get the best price possible or donations from local caterers, restaurants, food wholesalers, and grocery stores. The more that is donated, the more the price of the ticket or the sale of a food item goes directly to the fundraiser. Also, some of your friends, who may be bakers or home chefs, might be willing to cook up some fantastic items for sale. Cookies, brownies, cakes, muffins, pies, frozen home-made lasagnas, chicken pot pies, and casseroles would all be huge hits and guaranteed to make lots of money at a festival.

For our school festival, we would likely sell a lunch that would consist of a choice of hamburger or hotdogs, a bag of chips, and a drink for $5. Any sort of special dessert would be extra.

Tap into everybody's resources to see who has great food connections. Does anybody have a source for a donation of bottled water? Is the grocery store manager a friend of a friend who can donate buns, ketchup, and mustard? Get together a team to go out into the community and ask for food donations.

Our sample cause, the family festival, does not charge admission, so all money will be made through donations, food sales, and extras such as bouncy castles and face painting.

If you are planning on charging for admission, give careful thought to the demographics of the people who will be coming to your event. What is a reasonable amount for your neighborhood, considering what they will be getting? Be sensitive to the amount that people can afford.

You will need an activity committee to start thinking about the events of the day, which we will discuss next.

Planning Out The Activities of the Day

Now it's time to start thinking about the structure of your event. Get your committee to start thinking about what kinds of activities will keep guests interested in sticking around as long as possible. Formal affairs usually include a silent auction, cocktails, a band, speakers, dinner or hot hors d'oeuvres, and a live auction. A band, a caterer, and a live auctioneer would need to be booked.

Informal events could have ongoing activities that are staggered throughout the party. For an outdoor festival, you could figure out a niche attraction that is unique to your community. For instance, I grew up in Amish country, and the Amish are famous for their baked goods. A stand featuring Amish baked goods would be a huge way to generate income for the event. In Charlotte, where I live now, we are known for our North Carolina barbeque, and having a BBQ pit stand would be fun. If you are in a place with abundant fresh produce, like California or Florida, a fresh fruit and vegetable stand or farmer's market stand might make sense.

Try and connect with the local sports teams and arts organizations in your area. Are there pro or college teams close to you? If so, perhaps you can speak to a representative to invite some of the players to come out on behalf of the team, or maybe they have some signed team jerseys or donated tickets that can be auctioned. The same can be true for the arts community. Tickets to the symphony or ballet can be donated, and perhaps performers can come by to perform or sign programs.

In our test event, professionals who benefited from school arts and sports programs growing up should be willing to support the children who are at risk of not getting that training.

For our festival, we would need to think about what families would enjoy doing with their kids. There could be face painters, magicians, balloon artists, bouncy castles, and possibly the high school band. The local fire and police stations and EMTs might work with you to bring some squad cars and trucks so that kids could get comfortable meeting them, play with the sirens, and sit in the seats. The school's sports teams should be out circulating to help collect money, or perhaps they could sit in a dunking booth. After all, who wouldn't want to dunk the coach, quarterback, or linebacker?

For music, you might be able to get a local radio station to come to your event, or an on-air personality from radio or TV could emcee parts of your event.

A structure for our sample festival event might look like this:

10-2 food
10-12 pony rides
10-2 magicians
11-1 silent auction
12:30 –2 train rides
1-2 live auction
10-2 balloon artists
10-2 craft corner
10-2 rotating musical entertainment

Getting Kids Involved

No matter the event, children can help out with the many tasks that need to be accomplished to pull off the big day. Assemble a group and brainstorm with them to get ideas for entertainment, food, and revenue. What would they like to see? What can they help with? Guide them if they are having trouble getting started, but it's likely that their enthusiasm and imagination will bring new ideas to the table.

For our school festival example, it's so important that the schoolchildren whose lives will be impacted by this fundraiser are given a forum to discuss goals and thoughts. They need their voices to be heard. Kids might suggest making special t-shirts to sell with the day's logo on them, with the idea of wearing them during football season on spirit day. They'll want the school newspaper and yearbook organizer to cover the event. Those who run spirit events might have great ideas.

Details, Details, Details

Think about seating. If you are having a sit-down dinner, are there enough tables and chairs, tablecloths, and so forth? If this is a more informal day, do you need places for people to sit and rest, as well as tents in case the heat or the sun is intense? If you are having an outside event, you need to have sunscreen for people – perhaps that can be donated or underwritten by an area dermatologist or family doctor.

You will need to worry about cash flow. Are there any expenses coming up that you are going to have to pay for in order to get the equipment or food or location you need? See if these items can be billed after the event. If that's not an option, maybe you can go to a few folks on your committee, pool some money, and reimburse everyone when the event is over.

Consider finding corporate sponsors. Look around the

community and determine who might make a direct donation to the cause to help underwrite any expenses. Look at themes that would tie to that event, and think of businesses that might fit in well with what you are doing. For our theoretical event, we could go to sporting goods stores, music stores, and any service company that works with kids (pediatricians, orthodontists, orthopedists, tutoring houses, etc.).

Be strategic: if you decide you're going to have a live auction – you might find a willing orthodontist happy to donate braces. There might be a travel agency who can donate a trip, or they might have airline tickets to donate. Review the destination vacations within a relatively close drive of where you live, and try to piece together a place to stay, a dinner, and entertainment for a getaway. One item that never fails to grab at the heart-strings and insures an exciting live auction – a dog donated from a local breeder or a rescue dog, complete with training and obedience lessons.

For raffles, flat screen TVs always do well, as do 50/50 tickets (50% of the cash goes to the winner, 50% goes to the charity). Think of ways that retail stores sell their items, - try to make it a better deal for the guests to buy more tickets. For instance the tickets could cost $3.00 each, or you could sell 2 for $5.00 and 5 for $10.00.

You'll want to make sure that your event is covered by insurance. For instance, our school festival would be on school grounds – we'd need to check with the principal to make sure that the fair would be covered.

If you are having an outdoor event, do you have plans in place for a rain-date? Should there be an EMT truck there in case someone has heat stroke or gets injured? You will also need to think about hiring security for any cash that you might have, to direct traffic, and to be there in case of mishaps. Talk to your local police station about what is needed in order to be safe.

Don't forget about bathroom breaks! Do your guests

have somewhere to go for the restroom? If you are having an outdoor event, you might have to worry about getting some port-a-potties. It's not glamorous, but it's a necessity.

Some people love to think about decorations and signage all day long. These might include balloons, colored tablecloths, streamers, flowers, cups, and plates. Think about everything you will need to make your area look festive and fun, and continue the theme around the event.

Local churches should be contacted to see if they are willing to get involved. They might have something that could be donated, like tables and chairs, or they might have a newsletter where they could inform their members of the event.

One great idea is to offer up an area for local non-profits to set up at your event to dispense information about their charities that might be related to your cause.

A local recreation center, such as a YMCA, might want to help you out. Some of their instructors could help with games, referee, or lend equipment. They may also be able to help you fill out your list of volunteers who can help on the day of the event.

Invitations

Invitations for formal events typically go out six weeks before an event. People on your list might get several black tie or cocktail invitations a year, and yours needs to stand out, but don't go overboard getting the most elegant. Those potential attendees and donors might get upset if the invitation you sent looks like you spent too much money on it, given that you're supposed to be raising money for a charity. Make sure you've got somebody on your team with excellent taste to weigh all the options and negotiate with the printer for the best bang for the buck. Also factor in the cost of stamps and the time needed to address invitations.

For more informal events, get flyers up to get the word out, as discussed in Chapter 3. Take advantage of the internet to save on printing costs, and utilize "people power" to get the word out via email, Twitter, Facebook, etc.

Your invitation list is crucial to your success. Find out whether there is already a donor list available for your charity, and if there is none, network with your committee, friends, and neighbors in order to use theirs. Invite the local government and state representatives. You never know who might be able to come – after all, this fundraiser will benefit their constituents.

Volunteers

Recruiting volunteers is an extremely important part of having a successful event because you can't do this alone. Every member of your committee should help with the recruitment of volunteers. Word should get out that volunteers are needed, as discussed in Chapter 3.

Write down lists of the different jobs to be filled for your event. Some of these responsibilities might include: set-up, silent auction tables (set-up and monitoring and distribution), food, registration and information table, donations table, raffle tickets seller, entertainment, and clean-up.

You will need a very organized person for your silent auction items. He or she needs to keep track of everything you have, know the retail value, and make bid sheets. Most people start bids at half of what they worth and increase by $5.00.

For the auctioneer, you want somebody with experience. This person will get people excited and raise as much money as possible. A few spotters are needed to see if people raised their hands. Those spotters should have clipboards so that when an individual has the winning bid, they are immediately taken care of; the payment can be made and the item given out.

A silent auction tent at a festival

It's great to have a volunteer who has a brain for logistics. These people can look at an open field or a warehouse space and figure out where everything should go. This person should then create a diagram so the design for every element of the event can be handed out to the volunteers for set-up.

A photographer can volunteer his or her time to take photos, and half of proceeds from any sale from her website can go back to the charity.

On the day of the event, hold a volunteer meeting to brief everyone before you get started. Make sure you have snacks for the volunteers to fuel them. Talk about specific responsibilities, explain where everything is located, and make sure they know exactly what the event is for and who is going to benefit. Have some sort of streamlined look for the volunteers – whether they have specific (donated) t-shirts, a uniform of all black, or a special pin or tag that says "Volunteer."

A volunteer coordinator is essential to make sure everyone is manning their stations, and this person can also act as a contact for any issues that rise up throughout the day.

The Big Day

You will need plenty of time to get yourself ready for the big day. Have your volunteers meet you early as well to get set up and in place.

When they walk in, people should be given some sort of flyer so that they know the schedule for the event. For instance, include times for the silent auction and live auction, when there are going to be presentations on the stage area, when food service begins, etc.

Use walkie-talkies to talk to some of the key volunteers. Have a list of events in front of you, and set your cell phone alarm to alert you in time for each new event.

After the Event

Have a wrap-up debriefing with your committee and any volunteers who are interested. What went well and what didn't? Is it worth it to do this again? Who wants to be on the planning team for next year? Look at your spreadsheets – analyze what worked well to generate revenue and what did not. If this event is going to be repeated, it's good to keep notes to remember for the next time.

Thank-you cards should go out to all volunteers and donors. If you had a formal event, send thank-you notes to attendees who bought tables or tickets. In this letter, let people know how much money they helped to raise. Be specific so they know exactly how the money will be utilized.

I hope you've had fun walking through many of the

logistics and details that need to be thought about when planning a fundraising event. There are likely many more plans that need to be discussed and deliberated for what you are working on. However, the success you will feel as you see people having fun as they contribute to a worthwhile cause will be worth all the unexpected bumps in the road. The ultimate accomplishment, of course, is getting people the funds they need to reach their goals.

After all, can't you picture all those happy kids being able to participate in sports, drama, and choir?

5 things you can do today
5 things you can do today
5 things you can do today
5 things you can do today
5 things you can do today
5 things you can do today
5 things you can do today
5 things you can do today
5 things you can do today
5 things you can do today

5 things you can do today

Spotlight: Arts and Sports Programs

With budgets cut to fund arts and sports programs in public schools throughout the country, here are some ways to make a difference:

1. Ask your friends, family, and colleagues to donate instruments or sporting equipment.

2. See if you can get a local professional musician to come into the school and give a motivational speech/recital.

3. Ask students to bring $1 to wear baseball hats or flip-flops to school, and they can put the proceeds toward the equipment fund.

4. Help initiate one of the sports teams at school to organize a car wash.

5. Make calls today to have a fundraising concertconcert fundraiser, featuring the schools performers with band, choir, orchestra, glee club, and garage bands.

chapternine
chapternine
chapternine
chapternine
chapternine
chapternine
chapternine
chapternine
chapternine
chapternine
chapternine

Our Mission To Inspire Others

We all have talents and abilities that others can use. By calling on colleagues and friends to pitch in, a chain reaction of giving and volunteering can occur.

One of the things I do is travel around the country and share this message of helping change the world for the better. I was speaking in Dallas, Texas, and a woman named Lesley was in the audience who was so energized by what I shared. When she went to Walmart that night to run an errand, she found her own opportunity to make a difference.

Lesley

"A woman, her husband, and two kids (young girl and boy) were in line in front of me at Walmart. She had her money stacked on the counter; she knew exactly how much she had, and she was adding in her head what the total would be. It ended up being more than what the woman had. She said to the cashier, "Take this off," (eggs), "Take this off," (cans of tomato sauce), "Take this off." **We are talking about $4.00.** I am looking at this little girl, and she is looking at me. At this point, I looked in my somewhat empty wallet and found $4.00. I handed her the $4.00 and said, "Take this." Of course she said, "No." I said, "Take it." I am thinking to myself, "Today I have $4.00, but tomorrow I may not." She took the money and hugged me. Then the little girl hugged me, and the husband mouthed, "Bless you." I felt good about doing this. I don't think I will forget that woman and her family. I shop in Walmart weekly, and I will look for them."

Rather than looking the other way when this family needed help, Lesley stepped in because this family's plight pulled on her heartstrings. She knew she could help.

As you can see from Lesley's example, people feed off of each other's energy, and their stories inspire others to make a difference. We feel a band of solidarity because we all experience the same type of feeling when we help each other. Whether you do something large or small, **helping somebody feels good**. It shows that your presence on this Earth can make a real difference.

Helping somebody shows that your presence on this Earth can make a real difference.

Every single one of us has a story of a time when we helped somebody. My website, www.dontchangethechannel.com, is filled with narratives from ordinary people who have shared their stories of giving or receiving kindness. It is my hope that the site is a life-affirming and inspirational place to visit, and it will hopefully empower people to create more possibilities. The depth and range of experiences that are posted on the site are awesome.

For instance, I never expected a man to write in about preventing a stranger from jumping off a bridge.

Daryl

"I was running a few weeks ago in uptown Charlotte and was headed across a large bridge over a major highway. As I crossed the bridge, I noticed a young man standing in the middle. He had his hood up, and his pants were baggy. I could not see his face, but I thought that he might be laughing on the phone by the sounds he was making. As I got closer, I noticed that his foot kept lifting to the railing, and that he was not laughing but crying. I passed by him and then stopped. I turned back and said: "Are you ok?" He shrugged me off and tried to move away. After a few minutes of convincing, he opened up to me, telling me that he was 18 years old, and his parents had left him with his sister a long time ago. His parents did not care, and his sister had a family and did not have time for him. He told me that he was only happy for one minute every day, and the rest of the day he was miserable."

"Quickly, I came up with a mission for him. I told him he needed to go to a church. I suggested that God was not the reason he should go. Instead, I told him to go and talk to the clergy and find out in what ways he can help people. I suggested taking meals to the elderly or serving in a kitchen. The main goal was just to help people as much as you can for the next six months. Next, I told him to find me after those six months, and tell me if he had found any joy that he had been missing. After I walked him off the bridge and told him the location that he can find me at work, he gave me a big smile and said, "I will see you in six months. Thanks so much.""

Not everyone will come across a person on a bridge thinking of jumping, let alone have the courage and ability to stop a possible suicide. When I first saw this story on the site, my gut reaction was: What if this is seen by someone who has a friend or family member who is having suicidal thoughts, and this gives them inspiration to potentially save someone's life?

Here's another amazing story that might make you wonder what you would do if a co-worker was sick and needed help. Would you ever be willing to give an organ to a colleague?

Lisa

"In 1998 I was diagnosed with polycystic kidney disease (PKD for short), which is life-threatening. Cysts grow on your kidneys, completely take them over, and destroy your kidney function. When my kidney function dropped down to about 25%, I was told I would have to go on dialysis. Baptist Hospital in Winston-Salem, NC, where I was being treated, gave me packets to have potential donors send in to be tested for a match. When I was giving out the packets, my boss asked me where his was. He had told me when I was first diagnosed with PKD that he would donate one of his kidneys to me. I didn't take him seriously. To make a long story short, he completed one of the packets, sent it back in, and was a match. They told me at the hospital, "When we test to see if someone matches, we check six antigens, and if we find even one match out of six we can still do a transplant." My boss, Chris, and I matched THREE out of six. On May 28, 2007, we were admitted to the hospital, and on May 29th the transplant took place. Chris is doing well, and I feel the best I have felt in years. Talk about an answer to prayer and a wonderful blessing."

This courageous story might make someone feel differently about signing up to be on a bone marrow list or helping a family member who is on dialysis.

Have you ever been on the other end of a phone conversation when you heard something you would immediately volunteer for?

Sarah

"I was a morning radio host in Charlotte, NC, for 10 years. About eight years ago I answered the phone in the studio one day. It was a listener, Teresa, who had heard me talking about Charlotte's Susan G. Komen Race for the Cure. Teresa had just been diagnosed with breast cancer and was pretty scared about her upcoming chemotherapy. I asked if she wanted some company during her treatments, and a few days later I was sitting next to her as she got her chemo. We became good friends, and I joined her for her treatments as often as I could. Last month Teresa learned that her cancer has returned. I'm ready for more long talks and shared Popsicles in the chemo room if she wants me there."

Sometimes a simple phone call can spur somebody on to action, but the action is nothing dramatic – just holding hands and being there during a scary time.

Getting the Word out to Adolescents

I knew we needed to get kids involved in *Don't Change the Channel.* Working with kids and schools has become a major part of what we are trying to accomplish.

Adolescents get very caught up in the drama and emotions of being a teen, so much so that stories of good will quickly get tossed aside in lieu of the latest scandal (even grown-ups are prone to this!). Most adolescents are really good kids deep down, but in groups they can be mean and destructive towards each other. These are the kids who need to not only be reminded of the power of kindness, but they also need to be immersed in it on a daily basis. Adolescents need to be exposed to stories in the classroom that allow **them** to realize that there is so much more to who they are than just drama and chaos.

This observation of mine – sharing stories of making a difference helps people - got magnified tenfold when I asked a friend whether she thought she could get her students involved with the *Don't Change the Channel* movement. Sarah is a teacher of 8th graders, most of whom are 13 years old. Here is what happened when she shared my story of *Don't Change the Channel* with her class.

"My name is Sarah McKenna, and I teach 8th grade Science at Randall Middle School in Lithia, FL. I really wanted to spend more time with my kids on "character education" and topics that would really impact their lives. About two-thirds of the way through the year, I got a call from Jenn. She explained what I might be able to do with my kids. I was all ears."

"At the beginning of each of my five classes on April 1, I sat down and told my kids that I needed their help. You may not know this about 13-year-olds, but when they hear that you need their help they drop everything so that they can do whatever you need them to do. I proceeded to tell them about my friend Jenn and about the kind of person she is. For probably the first time in my four-year teaching career, I had all eyes on me, unwavering. By the time I got to the story of Blake, they were hooked! Most of my kids were visibly moved by the situation. I told them all the amazing things that Jenn did for Blake and his family. By now I'd been talking to them for about 15 minutes, and they still hadn't looked away once. They couldn't believe that one person, much less a person that their science teacher knew, could accomplish so much for someone she didn't even know."

"From there I showed the kids Jenn's website and explained that Jenn wanted to provide a forum for people to share their stories. I told them that most people weren't able to do something as monumental as what Jenn had done for Blake. What makes life so great, however, is the small things we do everyday that we may not even think about. I shared some of my own "everyday" stories of kindness with my kids, so that they could then start to relate some of their own experiences to acts of kindness and see that we all do little things everyday to perpetuate kindness. Once we had navigated her site, the kids begged me to read some of the stories people had submitted."

"Then the hands started going up. 'This one time....' or 'When I was a kid....' or 'I know someone who....' They had so many stories to share. I handed out index cards to the students and asked them to write one anonymous story on the card. It could be something they did for someone else, something someone did for them or their family, or something that they had witnessed that inspired them on the card. Some kids asked for a second card to either continue their story or to share a second story. There was not one negative comment the entire time we discussed this topic. For 8th graders, that is a HUGE accomplishment!"

"I'd known these kids for close to eight months, and I was shocked at some of the things they were going through that I had no idea about. If it weren't for an opportunity like this one to share all the "good things" going on in our lives, I may never have known what some of my kids were dealing with. I would not have known how grateful they were for the things people did for them and how willing they were to do something nice for someone else."

"We then put together a *Don't Change the Channel* bulletin board to display all the stories for our whole school to read!"

"What an amazing and inspirational experience to share with my kids. I feel that I know them so much better now, and I feel that they all will be on the lookout for their chance to not "change the channel". This could very likely be the **one** experience they remember from their middle school years, and I'm so proud to have been a part of it!"

When Sarah sent me those 120 stories, I was awe-struck. It was amazing to think about all the things that those kids had done and had done for them. It was so exciting to hear that this age group had gotten motivated and excited about

Sarah McKenna and I in front of the display made from the students'
stories for Don't Change the Channel

being kind to each other. When I read their accounts, I knew I had to go to Florida and visit these kids. I wanted to thank them in person.

My day at Randall Middle School was an emotional, empowering and uplifting day. I saw kids wanting to do the right thing and thinking it was cool to do so. A girl told me she had been struggling with thoughts of suicide. When she read the website, though, she was able to see life through the eyes of the people who had written in; it gave her hope. This powerful conversation with that thirteen-year-old let me know that we were on the right track with the outreach of *Don't Change the Channel*.

I memorized all 120 stories, so I knew everyone – the kids were blown away by how I had done this, but I wanted to show how important they were to me. Here is a small

Talking to the 8th grade classes at Randall Middle School

sample of some of the stories that came out of the class of thirteen-year-olds in Florida:

"We helped a homeless person by giving them food, money, and dog food for their dog."

"A few weeks ago, my acting coach put together a fundraiser for this kid named Liam. He has leukemia, and his parents didn't have enough money to pay for his medical bills. People came to the fundraiser and bought tickets to an upcoming show. We raised over $2,000!"

"On September 9, 2004, I lost my dad. He had been coaching a football team for the Mini League Super Bowl all year long. The team members and families knew about our financial situation after the funeral fees. They set up a fundraiser to help us get by financially, and we are forever thankful."

"I came home one night from church and found the

house looking tastefully clean. I walked around the house, and no one was downstairs. So I went upstairs, and my sister was reading in bed. Before she went to sleep I asked her why the house was so clean and she yelled, 'RAK'EM!' I said, 'What?' She said, 'Random Acts of Kindness.' I was very thankful for a break from cleaning the house."

I talked to all five of Sarah's classes that morning, and then I sat individually with each of the students to learn about them.

We talked about the power of their stories and about the impact a lesson like this had on them. We brainstormed projects that they could get involved with over their summer break.

I had a fantastic day at Randall Middle School. I am so excited about all of the new schools that are going to be taking on this curriculum as part of their school year. There are

This photo sums up our whole day together – the children are with the posters and banners they made for my visit for Don't Change the Channel.

Because I have red hair and freckles, I gathered together everyone who had red hair and/or freckles for a group photo. This is one of my favorite photos of the day.

so many terrific kids out there working to become a tremendous generation for effecting positive change.

The Smallest Helpers Get Involved

I know that even the smallest people in our communities, those in elementary school, should be taught at an early age that giving to others can make a huge difference to people. One of the teachers I reached out to is a friend from Ohio. Here is her story.

"My name is Jennifer, and I teach second grade in Akron, Ohio. Recently, Jenn contacted me to see if I could help her get the second grade perspective on helping others.

I thought it would be beneficial to begin by reading books on the topic, and then talking about scenarios and how they would react to them. I then posed the question, "How do you show kindness?"

"Second graders are always willing to tell you just about everything, so they were very eager to share their thoughts. After answering the question in a group, I had them answer the question again on paper. They illustrated their writing, and I displayed their kind thoughts on the bulletin board and around the classroom. I told them that even though they are seven and eight years old, they too can change the world by helping those in need."

"We then read about the eighth graders in Florida who conducted this same type of lesson in their school. The students were eager to hear what the "big kids" had to say, so I read a few of the comments that I knew the second graders could relate to. As I read, my students all had their hands up wanting to share more and more ways that they show kindness to others. I encouraged the students to go home, discuss the lesson, and visit the website with their parents."

"This lesson has impacted my students immensely. I see them looking out for each other more. They are more willing to go the extra mile to help their classmates and others around school. When a student drops crayons on the floor, ten students race over to help pick them up instead of one. If a student forgets to close their locker, another child closes it. Chairs needing to be pushed in are no longer being ignored. The students are quick to offer their glue sticks or erasers to someone who doesn't have one. I can see the wheels turning in their heads when they notice someone is sad or angry. They walk over to see how they can make that person feel better."

As teachers, parents, and citizens we have a responsibility to teach empathy and kindness, as well as show the benefit of this through our actions toward others.

Evolution of *Don't Change the Channel*

What began as a fundraiser in my hometown has since grown into a movement that evolves everyday. The stories featured here show that if we can continue to harness the untapped energy of enormous groups of people to do good in the community, it could benefit so many worthy causes.

While I could never have imagined the way *Don't Change the Channel* has evolved, it is so exciting to think of the future. where people no longer move their eyes away from someone who needs help on the street, and no longer change the channel on a cause that needs a champion.

5 things you can do today
5 things you can do today
5 things you can do today
5 things you can do today
5 things you can do today
5 things you can do today
5 things you can do today
5 things you can do today
5 things you can do today

5 things you can do today

Spotlight: Getting Off the Couch and Out of the House

There are so many children and adults overweight and at risk for serious health problems such as diabetes, heart disease, and more. Help encourage everyone you know to step away from the couch, and into learning habits that will make them healthier.

1 Put together a team to walk together after work and homework at night.

2 Have some kids over to a once a month cooking night for healthy meals, and bring home recipes for the whole family.

3 Become a clearinghouse of information about all the great after-school activities there are going on in the community, and help drive carpools if needs.

4 Help kids organize a field day in the neighborhood where they invent games, get timers, and win prizes.

5 Take a vote on which charity walk your friends want to get involved with, and start raising money for your team.

chapter ten
chapter ten
chapter ten
chapter ten
chapter ten
chapter ten
chapter ten
chapter ten
chapter ten
chapter ten
chapter ten

Once You Get Started, You Just Can't Stop

Once we surprised Blake's family with their house, the next several months were spent feverishly renovating. Our goal was to have a move-in date of before Thanksgiving 2007. We wanted the family to be able to enjoy their first Thanksgiving dinner together in their new house. Over the next four months, the renovation was a work in progress. Lenny Huddleston (see his story in Chapter 4) had put a team of 120 people together who had volunteered their time to work on this project.

Every time I flew home to see the work that was done, I could never get through a conversation with one of the volunteers without crying. Watching all of these volunteers work at night and on the weekends, giving up time with their families, was an emotional experience for me. See-ing the sacrifice that Lenny Huddleston made to make this dream home a reality was inspiring; Lenny put his whole self into this project. Every time there was a need for the house, it seemed like it was magically granted. The contractors got whatever was needed through volunteers.

That October, I was having a lunch meeting with some-one who worked for American Express. During the course of our conversation, she happened to tell me that she was from

Cincinnati, and her daughter had just moved to Uniontown, Ohio. "That's where I'm from!" I said. I started to share how the community of Uniontown had rallied around Blake and his family. She was very aware of the whole story. At the end of the lunch, she told me how her mother had died four years earlier from cancer. Every Christmas since her mother's passing, she and her husband picked out a charity to which they would donate $500. Although we had just met and spent only 45 minutes together at lunch, she decided that Blake's house would be a great recipient of their donation. I was thrilled!

When I shared this news with other people, checkbooks came flying out! We raised several thousand dollars that month, and with that money we were able to help buy furnishings for their house.

The day we had all been waiting for had finally arrived: it was time for Blake's family to move into the house. We wanted to make that heart-rending move a very uplifting time for the family, as well as for everyone involved in the renovations. To make the first viewing of the house even more exciting, we had the family put on blindfolds so they couldn't see the house until we got up close. Ann Kagarise and I walked the family up to the top of the driveway. The driveway was lined with business owners who had donated materials, goods, and services for the building of the house. When the blindfolds came off, they got to see their finished home, as well as all of the people who had worked so hard to make it beautiful. Lenny Huddleston proudly gave them the keys to the house, and they walked in to see the house complete for the very first time.

Several news teams from area TV stations had arrived to cover the event live for the 6:00 news. I'll never forget when we went into the kitchen; Blake's grandmother was admiring all the beautiful work that had been done. There were new countertops, cabinets, appliances, and a pantry packed with

Representatives from Countrywide Mortgage and the Portage and Summit
County Home Builders Association who helped to donate and rebuild the house
for Blake's family

food. I was standing at the back of the kitchen, watching several reporters and a sea of people crowd into the room. As Blake's grandmother looked around, a reporter asked, "What does this mean to you?" She replied, "This means six people don't have to live in a two bedroom apartment anymore." At that moment, her eyes found me in the back of the room. She looked me square in the face and mouthed, "Thank you." I felt like everything we had worked so hard on had finally come together for this family.

The tour continued throughout the house. We came to the laundry room. The washer and dryer were donated by five families who had teamed up to do a garage sale; the proceeds went to buy these appliances. These families might not have realized how big a deal it was for them to have donated the washer and dryer, but Blake's family had always had to go to a Laundromat, pockets stuffed with quarters, to get their family's laundry done. Now they had a dedicated laundry room right in the house.

There was so much love and celebration around the house. It was pure joy for everyone to see the kids in the backyard swinging on their new playset, sliding down the slide, and going back and forth on the monkey bars. I was so happy for them; even though we couldn't take away their suffering, at least we were able to put a smile on their faces and bring them some joy with this home.

It's a night that will stay with me the rest of my life.

The celebrations continued that night with a thank-you dinner nearby for everyone who had worked so hard on the house. Two hundred people had been involved in making the house a reality. When you show your appreciation for people who have helped, they search for other projects to work on.

I asked the Cleveland Browns if there was any way to get tickets for the final game of the year for the 120 people who helped construct the house. They generously agreed. Leigh Bodden, a starting defensive back for the Browns, came to the dinner to surprise the volunteers. He brought bumper stickers, t-shirts, and autographed pictures. Leigh was so gracious with his time, making a point to talk to everyone and take photos.

One of the construction workers who had worked on the house came up to me, with tears in his eyes, and told me how excited he was to go to a Cleveland Browns game. Never in his life had he been to a professional sporting event. He felt validated and appreciated for the work he had done. He was so proud of what they had done, and it was clear that this would not be the last time he was going to volunteer. He was inspired to do more.

Over the next several days, I replayed that Monday night in my mind. I couldn't believe how all the pieces of the puzzle had fallen into place to make that beautiful house become a reality. I've never had a more meaningful Thanksgiving holiday in my life.

The Saturday after Thanksgiving was the first time in five months when all that we had done began to sink in. As I was standing in my bathroom drying my hair, all the emails, conversations, letters, acts of courage, and kindness came flooding back to me. In this moment, it became clear that the story could not end here. Ordinary people do make extraordinary things happen. We all have it in us to change the world. I do believe that God has blessed us all with an amazing gift of this lifetime, and it is our responsibility to honor him and do as much as we can to serve others. I wanted to share with people the compassion, the coming together to make a difference, and the love that is carried in peoples' hearts. That love is just waiting for an opportunity to be showered on another, so give them the tools they need to go out there and get started today.

It was an exhausting five months, and you may wonder, what fuels us to do it again? I think it is the difference people see in the faces of the people they are helping, the emotions they feel, and seeing their hard work pay off.

One of my favorite stories is from June Lambert. You may remember her from Chapter One. She was my neighbor in Ohio who had been in that terrible car crash and had limited mobility. But her enthusiasm for Blake's Bright Tomorrow gave her energy to overcome her physical limitations and become a major force in making our fundraiser a success. This work gave her purpose, something to believe in, and something to feel good about. In October of that year, she called to share some exciting news. She told me that she had walked a mile on the elliptical machine. It was a huge moment for her, as she had accomplished something that she

June Lambert on the elliptical machine

had not been able to do in over 10 years. June's kids and her husband told me how this volunteer work had completely changed her life.

I believe that once June had a project that she was passionate about, she was able to take her mind off her pain and really feel good about her accomplishments. I am proud to say that June continues to walks one to two miles a day on her elliptical machine.

It's not just about people who are struggling; it's about waking up everyday and doing your part to make this world a better place. Make a choice to have a spirit in you that always wants to help others. This spirit doesn't judge or discriminate – it helps anyone, anywhere, and in any situation.

A Dedication in Life

Lori DuBois had that spirit in her. Lori and I met eleven years ago when I was working in radio, and we became instant friends. Lori had an incredible energy that was infectious to everyone around her. You couldn't help but be drawn to her. She had a way about her that made everyone she touched feel excited about the gift of life.

Lori, unfortunately, wasn't able to have the gift of a long life. In 2002, at only 33 years old, she was diagnosed with ovarian cancer. She went into remission, but the cancer returned in 2007. The last few months of her life were a struggle for her, and we didn't get to talk as much as we normally would.

However, I was able to talk with her during one week, when she was feeling well and energetic. During some of our conversations she shared that she did not think she was going to beat cancer this time; she was at peace with that. I marveled at how happy and serene she was despite not knowing how much longer she had here on Earth.

It was very important to Lori to give a voice to other women who have to fight ovarian cancer. She found the Hera Women's Cancer Foundation that fall, and she talked to the director about the work they were doing and how she could help. It helped Lori to take the focus outside of herself and her battles. Even at the end of her fight, she wanted to give them that voice. I know how important that work was to her, down to her last day.

Lori loved to hear about all the stories we were collecting for *Don't Change the Channel*. She was excited about this project and our mission. I was honored to let her know that I was going to dedicate this book to her.

One day Lori called me after an uplifting experience she had at a gas station, of all places. When she went inside to pay, there was a long line at the counter. Lori was wearing two different colostomy bags in a pouch, which sometimes grew very heavy. A man who was close to the front of the line noticed her, and he said she could take his place in line. She was touched that a stranger had helped her out when she wasn't feeling well. While paying for the gas, she bought two lottery tickets to thank him. She turned around and gave him the tickets. He was so shocked and said, "How do I find you if we win?" She smiled and shook her head. "Nope - if you win all of the money is yours. This is a thank-you for letting me have your place in line," she said.

The story at the gas station, which Lori thought would be fun to include with the others in this book, illustrates so many points:

1 The kindness of a stranger who took action when he saw a woman who looked as though she needed a break from standing in line,

2 The joy that it gave Lori to be the recipient of a generous act,

3 The joy that it gave Lori to be generous in return.

Even though Lori was almost at her journey's end with life here on Earth, this encounter demonstrated to her how one person can make another's day just through a simple gesture. In a way, it reaffirmed to her the goodness of humanity.

Lori's story shows how human connections can inspire and give joy to all involved. Lori battled her cancer until the very end; she never gave up or lost hope. She was a warrior in every sense of the word.

We all need people like Lori in our lives who can inspire us to be better people and do better work. If you don't have a person like Lori who shows you how the common decency in humanity connects us all, then it's time to get out there and meet him or her.

Take Away

Lori never stopped caring about helping others, even in her final months. Whether you have been involved with the community all your life or are just beginning, it's important to know that when you're involved in moments of kindness, they'll fuel you to want to make this world a better place.

You want this feeling of involvement to be a part of who you are. Go through life with the awareness that you can help. Be available even on your busiest of days, and let your heart be open to what's going on around you.

Acknowledgments

acknowledgments
acknowledgments
acknowledgments
acknowledgments
acknowledgments
acknowledgments
acknowledgments
acknowledgments
acknowledgments
acknowledgments
acknowledgments
acknowledgments

It has been an amazing journey writing this book for the past three years. I am so blessed to have such wonderful family and friends who have supported this project from day one. Mom and Dad, thank you for adopting me. I have been so fortunate in life because you chose me. Thank you for always telling me I could do anything in life. Thank you for showing me how hard work, discipline and dedication can bring about many amazing results. You are my biggest cheerleaders and I love you dearly. Kristin, thank you for being my sister, and for all of your support throughout this project.

Chuck Hood, where do I even start? I love you dearly. This project would not have happened without you. Thank you for believing in me six years ago. Thank you for taking a chance on me. Everyday you allow me to run a business that would not be possible without you. Thank you for the time you have granted me over the past three plus years to work on Blake's Bright Tomorrow and writing this book.

Lou Solomon, I could never ask for a better mentor. You are such an inspiration to me. Thank you for your coaching and friendship.

To all of my Hood Hargett Breakfast Club family. Each

of you are so special to me. You make me proud each day to come to work and you constantly push me to be better.

Patty, Blake, Whitney, Audrey, Jane, Caylon and David. It breaks my heart the reason why we walked into each others' lives, but I feel so blessed to know and love each of you very much. I am honored to call you family.

Lou, Joe and Kara at LA Management, thank you for all of your talent and time you have put into this project. I am so proud to work with you! Kent at Pure Creative: your mind amazes me and I am always in awe of your talent. Thanks to Erin Malone, my copyeditor, and Angela Harwood, my designer – you've made my book read and look so beautiful.

Mike Minter, my life changed the day you walked in. You are such a gift to me.

I have the most amazing group of girlfriends: Angela, Jennifer, Marcy, Laura, Erica, Kathy, Jodie, Debbie, Cantey, Carolyn, Sarah W., Stacia, Candy and Sarah M. You make me proud to know each of you and I have no words for the support you have given to me.

Betsy, I have run out of words to describe you! Simply put, no way would I have a book without you. I learn from you everyday. Your wisdom, insight and talent to write is tremendous. Thank you for being my ghost writer, I love you.

resources
resources
resources
resources
resources
resources
resources
resources
resources
resources
resources
resources

Resources

Chapter One

Blake's Bright Tomorrow: www.blakesbrighttomorrow.com
Big Brothers Big Sisters: www.bbbs.org

Chapter Two

March of Dimes: www.marchofdimes.com
American Red Cross: www.redcross.org
Bill and Melinda Gates Foundation: www.gatesfoundation.org
Alzheimer's Foundation: www.alzfdn.org
Make-A-Wish Foundation: www.wish.org

Chapter Three

Children's Miracle Network: www.childrensmiraclenetwork.org
Give Kids the World: www.gktw.org

Chapter Four

Leukemia and Lymphona Society: www.leukemia-lymphoma.org
Habitat for Humanity: www.habitat.org
Dress for Success: www.dressforsucces.org

King's Kitchen: www.kingskitchen.org
Café Reconcile: www.reconcileneworleans.org
Rotary Club Charlotte: www.charlotterotary.org
Hood Hargett Breakfast Club – Liz Murray Scholarship Fund:
www.hoodhargettbreakfastclub.com

Chapter Five

Hattie Larlham Foundation – www.hattielarlham.org
Doughjangles – www.doughjangles.com

Chapter Six

Pet I Care: www.duke.edu
Duke Lemur Center: www.lemur.duke.edu
Starlight Society: www.lchchildrensfund.org
Crisis Assistance Ministry: www.crisisassistance.org
Wounded Warrior Project: www.woundedwarriorproject.org
Special Olympics: www.specialolympics.org
Med Assist: www.medassist.org

Chapter Seven

Police Activities League: www.nationalpal.org
Peace Corps: www.peacecorps.gov
Goodwill: www.goodwill.org
Juvenile Diabetes Research Foundation: www.jdrf.org

Chapter Eight

Susan G. Komen Foundation: www.komen.org

Chapter Ten

Hera Women's Cancer Foundation: www.herafoundation.org